SPECIAL PRAISE FOR

Life's Last Gift

"In this finely written and immensely useful book, Charles Garfield offers all of us the concrete guidance we'll need to skillfully and compassionately support those we love at the end of their lives. Dr. Garfield knows the terrain intimately and his book will help family members and friends of the dying negotiate this difficult and confusing time with grace and kindness."

—DAVID SHEFF, New York Times bestselling author
of *Clean* and *Beautiful Boy*

"Caring for someone during the last months of life is among our most profound—and daunting—responsibilities. Drawing skillfully on decades of professional experience and his own personal relationships, Charles Garfield imparts his practical wisdom to transform caring for a dying person from a problem to be solved to a journey to be walked, shoulder to shoulder, with the other. In *Life's Last Gift*, the path Garfield offers is the way of the heart."

—IRA BYOCK, MD, palliative care physician,
author of *Dying Well* and *The Four Things That Matter Most*

"Dr. Garfield has written a highly practical and useful book—packed with moving stories, deep wisdom, and inspiring insights. This accessible volume is a genuine gift that demonstrates how we can all be effective, supportive caretakers for the dying."

—ROGER WALSH, MD, PhD, professor of psychiatry,
UC Irvine Medical School, and author of
Essential Spirituality: The Seven Central Practices

"*Life's Last Gift* is a masterpiece of caregiving wisdom! It is a legacy of ideas and some of the most vital information I've ever read on dying—and living. Dr. Garfield's beautifully written book is a wise and loving work that you won't be able to put down; it belongs on every adult's required reading list."

—JIM SANTUCCI, executive director of
Kara: Grief Support for Children, Teens, Families, and Adults

"For decades, Charles Garfield has been a leader in the compassionate care of loved ones at the end of life. His moving teachings show us how we can open our hearts and minds and bring peace and fulfillment to the person who is dying and to all those who are affected. This is a rare and remarkable book, one that all of us will need. It is a genuine blessing!"

—KARIN EVANS, author of *The Lost Daughters of China*

"I am absolutely confident that Dr. Garfield's invaluable book *Life's Last Gift* will be important to you in your life. Its heartfelt and poignant stories and superb guidance offer us all a treasure trove of unique insights. This is a deeply compassionate work that speaks directly to all those who hope for greater peace and comfort at life's end."

—KAUSHIK ROY, executive director of Shanti Project: Enhancing the Health, Quality of Life, and Well-Being of People with Terminal, Life-Threatening, or Disabling Illnesses or Conditions

"*Life's Last Gift* is a distillation of wisdom gained from a lifetime of service in care of the dying. Dr. Garfield's authentic, eloquent sharing of personal experiences and guidelines for the reader make this book a heartwarming treasure to be read and shared with others right now, before it's too late."

—FRANCES E. VAUGHAN, PhD, author of *Shadows of the Sacred: Seeing Through Spiritual Illusions*

"Here is a book on end-of-life care that you will not be able to put down. *Life's Last Gift* offers family members, friends, and health professionals the support they need to navigate life's final chapter with grace, courage, and skill. It is a deeply honest work about dying, living, and loving. I recommend it enthusiastically."

—FRANK OSTASESKI, founder of the Metta Institute and author of *The Five Invitations: Discovering What Death Can Teach Us About Living Fully*

"Charles Garfield's book *Life's Last Gift* is a treasure. It is beautiful, heartfelt, and overflowing with hard-won, compassionate wisdom. My prayer is that it be offered in every hospice, hospital, and chaplaincy program—in every setting and to every person who will lovingly accompany someone at the end of life. My prayer is that my children will read it when it comes my time. This book is a gift."

—KATHLEEN DOWLING SINGH, author of *The Grace in Dying: How We Are Transformed Spiritually as We Die*

"*Life's Last Gift* is an inspiring and practical book of in-the-trenches caregiving wisdom. Readers will find a rare resource and a wealth of insight about life's end by a voice of experience and compassion. Dr. Charles Garfield has given health professionals, as well as family and friends of the dying, a unique gift of immense importance."

—MICKI KLEARMAN, MD, Genentech

"*Life's Last Gift*, itself a remarkable gift, shows us the healing power of conversations at life's end and offers us wisdom, courage, and guidance for having these challenging and heartfelt communications with those we love. Keep this book nearby, and don't wait to read it."

—DALE G. LARSON, PhD, professor of counseling psychology, Santa Clara University, and author of *The Helper's Journey: Working with People Facing Grief, Loss, and Life-Threatening Illness*

Life's Last Gift

Charles Garfield

LIFE'S
LAST
Gift

Giving and Receiving

Peace when a Loved One Is Dying

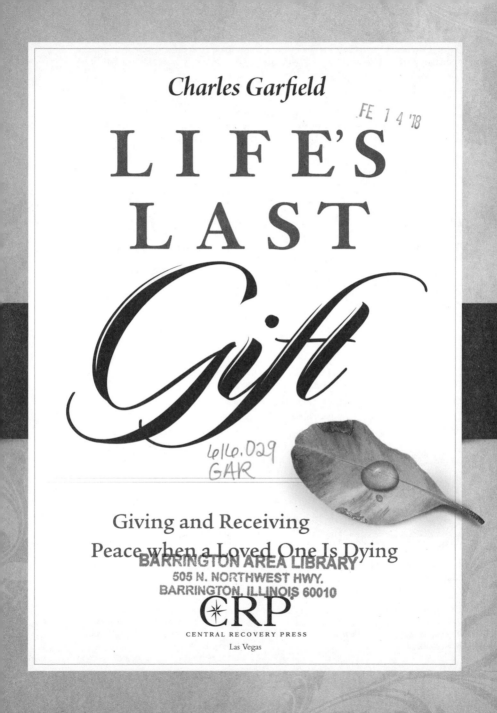

CRP
CENTRAL RECOVERY PRESS
Las Vegas

Central Recovery Press (CRP) is committed to publishing exceptional materials addressing addiction treatment, recovery, and behavioral healthcare topics. For more information, visit www.centralrecoverypress.com.

Publisher: Central Recovery Press
         3321 N. Buffalo Drive
         Las Vegas, NV 89129

22 21 20 19 18 17   1 2 3 4 5

Library of Congress Cataloging-in-Publication Data
Names: Garfield, Charles A., author.
Title: Life's last gift : how to give and receive peace when a loved one is dying / Charles Garfield.
Description: Las Vegas, NV : Central Recovery Press, [2017]
Identifiers: LCCN 2017020977 (print) | LCCN 2017034984 (ebook) | ISBN 9781942094517 (ebook) | ISBN 9781942094500 (pbk. : alk. paper) | ISBN 9781942094494 (hardcover : alk. paper)
Subjects: LCSH: Terminally ill--Psychology. | Death—Psychological aspects.|Peace of mind.
Classification: LCC R726.8 (ebook) | LCC R726.8 .G376 2017 (print) | DDC 616.02/9--dc23
LC record available at https://lccn.loc.gov/2017020977

Photo of Charles Garfield by Stu Selland. Used with permission.

Excerpts from "This Timeless Moment" and "O Nobly Born" from THIS TIMELESS MOMENT" A PERSONAL VIEW OF ALDOUS HUXLEY by Laura Huxley. Copyright © 1968 by Laura Archera Huxley. Reprinted by permission of Farrar, Straus, and Giroux.

This Timeless Moment: A Personal View of Aldous Huxley by Laura Huxley. Copyright © 1968, 2000 by Laura Archera Huxley. Used by permission of Georges Borchardt, Inc., on behalf of Laura Huxley. All rights reserved.

Republished with permission of CCC Republication from *Here and Now: Living in the Spirit*, Henri Nouwen. © 1994; permission conveyed through Copyright Clearance Center, Inc.

Excerpt from page 174 republished with permission of Kristin Neff from http://self-compassion.org.

Excerpt from page 212 republished with permission of Jan Thomas from "Music, Ministry and Spirit."

Every attempt has been made to contact copyright holders. If copyright holders have not been properly acknowledged, please contact us. Central Recovery Press will be happy to rectify the omission in future printings of this book.

Publisher's Note: This book contains general information about dying, hospice, caregiving, and related matters. The information is not medical advice. This book is not an alternative to medical advice from your doctor or other professional healthcare provider.

Our books represent the experiences and opinions of their authors only. Every effort has been made to ensure that events, institutions, and statistics presented in our books as facts are accurate and up-to-date. To protect their privacy, the names of some of the people, places, and institutions in this book may have been changed.

Cover and interior design and layout by Marisa Jackson.

FOR CINDY SPRING, WITH LOVE ALWAYS

61

Peace, my heart, let the time for the parting be sweet.
Let it not be a death but completeness.
Let love melt into memory and pain into songs.
Let the flight through the sky end in the folding
of the wings over the nest.
Let the last touch of your hands be gentle
like the flower of the night.
Stand still, O Beautiful End, for a moment,
and say your last words in silence.
I bow to you and hold up my lamp
to light you on your way.

—Rabindranath Tagore

Contents

QUICK GUIDE TO
Exercises & Guidelines

AUTHOR'S NOTE

I had no idea I would be writing *Life's Last Gift* while I was living most of the experiences I describe in the book, and, for the most part, I wasn't taking notes. So, I've drawn largely from memory of real-life situations. The stories I tell and people I describe reflect my current recollection of what we experienced years ago.

All quoted dialogue and comments are reconstructed from memory, not from transcriptions. I've tried to be true to the spirit and substance of what happened and to give an honest depiction of these experiences and events. The Shanti volunteers who share their stories are identified by their real names, but the names of most of the dying people, family members, and friends have been changed, as have many identifying details of their situations. Also, certain individuals are composites. Any similarity to persons living or dead resulting from these changes is completely coincidental and unintentional.

INTRODUCTION

It's easy to lose your bearings when someone you care about is dying. Even if you've been extremely close, a great divide opens with you on one side, in the kingdom of the well, and your loved one on the other, in the kingdom of the sick—the night side of life.

Roles blur as a friend or parent or lover becomes sicker and disappears into the startling and unfamiliar identity of "the dying one." Days fill with physical care and decisions that can't, ultimately, save this precious life. And we, who are well, look for guidance about what to say and how best to help. We're scared, anxious, and grieving, and we're desperate to offer support. But very often, we retreat emotionally—even in the midst of busily working for a "good death"—because it's so hard to stay present through the pain. We often know what to *do*—what tasks we need to perform—but we no longer know how to *be*.

I've watched this happen repeatedly in the four decades I've worked with dying people and their families, and I experienced it myself when caring for my father, mother, and best friend after they were diagnosed with terminal conditions. No matter how prepared we believe we are, I think most of us feel blindsided by what's asked of us as we try to comfort our loved ones and struggle to find the skill and grace that will help us reduce their pain.

This book will show you how to sustain emotional closeness when death enters the picture and help you nourish your relationship with the other person in ways that will allow your connection to deepen until the very end. In doing that, you'll find that you can bear the pain of your losses together and experience peace—even fulfillment—that you never could have had without each other.

In the chapters to come, I'll ask you to make a series of simple commitments about how you'll choose to be when you're with your loved one. These promises need never be spoken, but you can feel, understand, and act on them in ways that will help you stay focused and present. Each one will help you orient yourself, stay grounded, and keep offering meaningful support and compassion, even when you feel upset, confused, or lost.

I've used these essential guidelines to accompany hundreds of people through their dying time and to train many thousands of volunteers to do the same. They've helped countless people find a path to peace in the midst of turmoil. I began developing these guidelines in the 1970s as a psychologist at the Cancer Research Institute (CRI), which is part of the University of California Medical Center in San Francisco. There, in the days before there was a hospice movement in the United States, I was the sole staff member assigned to focus on the nonphysical needs of patients dying of cancer—their emotions, their spirits. I was particularly struck by the loneliness that was so much a part of life on the cancer ward. As people got sicker, their friends and families often stopped visiting, sometimes scared off by the symptoms or their own sadness, sometimes seeming to think that there was nothing they could do—so why visit at all? The few who came were likely to dance around the issue of death and would leave without ever really asking the person in the bed what he or she was thinking or feeling.

So much comes up emotionally and spiritually for people as their time runs short. They review their lives, forgive and ask forgiveness, and cycle through a wide spectrum of feelings in which they confront anger, sadness, fear, regret, joy, love, and the unanswerable question of what comes next. I realized that more than anything I could do as a professional, simply accompanying someone through that challenging emotional and spiritual vortex—human to human—had the most profound impact. So, I sat at bedsides, listening, talking, and witnessing the struggles, hopes, and stories of people who were about to die. In my years of doing that, I learned what helped them, what actions and attitudes made the biggest difference. Because the need was so great, and I was just one person, I founded an organization called Shanti to train volunteers to be with the dying, as I was doing. It later became San Francisco's first community-based agency supporting people with HIV/ AIDS, and it has served as a model for volunteer service groups in hundreds of communities around the world.

Shanti is a Sanskrit word that translates roughly as "the peace that surpasses understanding" or, more succinctly, "inner peace." Helping bring inner peace to the dying and those who care for them was—and is—a goal of Shanti volunteers. And, it's the goal of everything you'll find in this book.

Healing Without Cures

I want you to know that even in the thick of everything you're both facing, you can support your dying loved one in ways that create opportunities for greater independence and heartfelt connection as the hours and days count down. I've worked at close range with family members, lovers, and friends of the dying and consulted with thousands of health professionals and volunteers in hospitals, hospices, clinics, nursing homes, and the community. All of them discovered that greater peace at the end of life is a collective process. As my best friend Rico Jones put it shortly before he died, "It's all about relationships."

Being with your loved one now, and allowing yourself to have an honest, vulnerable relationship with him or her, requires skills that may be quite different from your usual ways of being around each other. You'll want to stay as present as possible in the time that's left, instead of checking out or holding onto expectations of how things should be. You may need to let go of old habits, such as fixing or giving advice or hiding your true feelings. The stories in this book, drawn from my own experiences and those of Shanti volunteers, will show you what works best as you support the other person now.

Family members, lovers, and friends—and people who were dying—have spoken to me candidly about the toughest parts of their experience, the choices and situations that had no obvious solutions, and the feelings of hopeless inadequacy. But, these same situations often became turning points for them as they learned to take heart-centered action and witnessed their care making a positive difference. They were able to find healing, even though it wasn't necessarily physical healing, and it happened not only for their dying loved ones but for them as well. You'll hear their voices, and have their wisdom and support, throughout this book.

I want you to know that if you're fighting to hold things together for yourself and your loved one, you are not alone. The people you'll meet in this book are with you. I'm with you. All of us have learned that some of the circumstances that befall us are outrageously painful and unfair, but they can trigger quantum leaps in our understanding of the meaning of our life and death. If we let it, the pain we face can open us to both giving and receiving greater expressions of caring and compassion. At a time of so much sadness and loss, we can find ourselves—and those we care about so much—filled with love.

This book is for you
if one of your loved ones has been
diagnosed with a life-threatening illness;
if you've just heard the bad news about a friend
or acquaintance and don't know what to do or say;
if you're contending with the ups and downs
of someone's cancer, heart disease, AIDS,
or potentially terminal condition;
if the prognosis is bleak, and you don't know

how to balance hope with the reality that time is short;
whether your heart is overflowing with love for the
other person right now, or you're caring for
someone who sets you on edge.

My hope and belief is that the insights and stories you'll read in the pages to come will help you find your center when your world is spinning and let you be the person you most want to be as you accompany someone through his or her last months and days.

My additional hope is that health professionals and volunteers who work with the dying, and, at times, constitute a kind of extended family, find encouragement to focus on caring as well as curing—being tough on problems yet tender with people.

There is one promise that dying people need to hear, more than any other, from those who love and care about them: *I choose to be with you in a healing partnership, though I know you're dying. I will stand with you in the midst of despair.*

I'd like to help you make this brave and comforting choice. It can be life's last gift.

Chapter One
I Will Listen from the Heart

THE 1ST COMMITMENT

I will listen to you from my heart, doing my best to still my racing thoughts and to hear what you are communicating to me. I will look into your eyes, breathe, and be fully present with you.

The dying time can be intensely isolating and lonely. Awkwardness, fear, and denial can untether even the closest relationships. Friends and family often retreat into panicked lists of "things we can do to save them," withdraw into sorrow, or muster false cheer and talk about how the person in the bed will be better soon.

When we fall into patterns like this, the dying are left alone with the reality of death. Amid all the words and interventions swirling around them, when death is not acknowledged, *they* are not acknowledged. They feel almost invisible. Abandoned.

That's why it's so important to turn your attention as fully as you can to what they're experiencing and go through it with them. Listening from the heart—which means letting yourself witness your loved one's words, emotions, and condition with love and without turning away—restores the connection that you long to have with each other.

I know the words that I'm using—*death, dying*—are extremely difficult to hear and absorb. When my father was diagnosed with advanced liver cancer and not expected to live more than six months, I struggled fiercely against what we all knew was true. Perhaps, if I didn't allow the word *death* to enter the conversation, it would go away. Perhaps, if I spent every free moment researching a cure, I'd discover something the doctors had overlooked. In my years of working with dying patients, it had always frustrated me to see their families shift into denial and magical thinking. They'd cling to the hope that loved ones would survive, even though they were in hospice, had lost forty or fifty pounds, and looked gaunt and drained. They'd often want their suffering loved ones to live "just a little while longer" or "until God sends a miracle." I was sure I would never do that, certain that I could face my own loved ones' dying time without avoiding the truth.

Yet, as Dad weakened, that's what I did. For weeks after his diagnosis, I disappeared into research that kept me constantly busy, in large part because I couldn't bear to sit still and simply be with him. I think I was frightened that I'd fall apart if I accepted what was happening, so I kept myself going, not wanting to feel, or to imagine what he was going through.

It wasn't until Dad gently let me know that he needed *me,* his son, not some treatment I might find, that I stopped running. And when I did, we could finally be honest with each other, *there* for each other.

Accepting our loved ones where they are, not where we want them to be, allows us to experience the closeness that can heal our hearts and theirs. Witnessing them, accompanying them through their journey toward death without trying to make it anything else, is the most meaningful gift you can give.

Your loved one is still living, and this is the final period of the life cycle, perhaps more precious than any other. When you stop yourself from pulling away and let the dying time be part of life and part of your relationship with the other person, you're saying, "You're still among us, one of us. We'll be in this together until the end. I promise you that."

Your willingness to listen from the heart gives value to the person inside the failing body and helps both of you shift your focus from what's the matter with him to what *matters* to him, what's true for him now. In sharing your loved one's pain, as you must to listen in this way, you offer a kind of companionship, and relief, that can come no other way.

The Roman Catholic theologian Henri Nouwen put it beautifully in his book *Out of Solitude* when he wrote,

> When we honestly ask ourselves which persons in our lives mean the most to us, we often find that it is those who, instead of giving much advice, solutions, or cures, have chosen rather to share our pain and touch our wounds with a gentle and tender hand. The friend who can be silent with us, who can stay with us in an hour of grief and bereavement, who can tolerate not knowing, not healing, not curing, and face with us the reality of our powerlessness, that is the friend who cares.

The value of all those "nots" has always impressed me deeply. For our loved ones at the end of life, there will very likely be no physical healing, no curing, no certainty except the certainty of death. But even then—*especially* then—our presence, our listening, can provide comfort and give value to life. Whatever we believe happens after death, we have a chance to give meaning to the hours right up to the end.

How to Listen from the Heart

AN EXERCISE

It's hard to be close to our loved ones' suffering. It's difficult even to walk into the room sometimes. We get scared off by so many things—the way the person looks now, the helplessness we feel when we see flashes of pain or confusion. The environment can seem daunting, too, with new smells, medicines, and equipment, along with intruding doctors and caregivers. It can feel overwhelming.

However, the techniques below have helped tens of thousands of people cope with the distress, so they can be there in a meaningful way for their loved ones. I'll talk you through the same instructions I've given to volunteers and family members. These are the tools that helped me every time I felt overwhelmed by the prospect of going to the bedside of a dying patient, which allowed me to bring the best of myself to my own loved ones when they were at the end of their lives. I promise you that they'll help you, too.

1. Stop at the Threshold

You can center yourself each time you visit by pausing at the threshold before you enter the room. Stand there quietly and breathe, slowly and deeply. With all the emotional and sensory overload you're experiencing, you may have lost your connection to your body. Come back by feeling your feet on the ground and sensing the breath moving in and out of your nostrils. Count *one* on the first slow inhale, *two* on the second. Count out ten deep, even breaths.

Remind yourself why you've come. It's not to impose an agenda, and it's not to make this whole situation go away. You can't. You're here to show your loved one that he or she doesn't have to go through this alone. One of the greatest fears of the dying is that they'll die by themselves, and your presence right now is a profound offering.

2. Get Close and Make Contact

Keep breathing, slowly and deeply, as you walk in. Pull a chair close to the bed. If it feels right, take the other person's hand and look into his or her eyes. There's no script to follow when you say hello. Keep it simple—I usually start with "How are you? How are things going for you today?" Then take your cues from the response that comes.

3. Keep Returning when You Drift

As you listen, hold the other person as the focus of a meditation. By that I mean tune in to your loved one, making regular eye contact and holding yourself in an attentive posture. Notice when your attention drifts away and keep bringing yourself back to your awareness of this other person in front of you.

You'll do this countless times in the space of a single visit because as you sit—absorbing the other person's voice and words, his or her body language and emotions—your mind is likely to run wild. The voices in your head respond to everything around and inside you, and they can easily drown out the voice that's speaking to you.

Your thoughts will likely range far and wide: "I'm so scared. What should I do? She looks so frail today. Why is this happening? How much longer do I have to stay? He's really off the wall. I have no idea what to say. I can't stand another minute of this. God, I'm so glad it's not me."

All of this is perfectly normal. Hindu teachers describe the mind as a drunken monkey lurching from thought to thought, hardly able to settle long enough to experience what's happening in this moment. You'll have thousands of thoughts and judgments. But with practice, and a commitment to keep listening from the heart, you can learn to stay present for longer and longer stretches, and as you get better at it, you're less likely to get blown out of the water by stories about excruciating medical treatments or by the tears and anger that may come with the memory of an ancient hurt. Your capacity for calmly listening to the tough stuff will expand each time you sit and breathe and pay attention to the other person.

4. Keep Breathing

It takes considerable courage for a dying person to talk about the nearness of death and reflect on the meaning, hopes, and regrets of a lifetime. It takes courage, too, to listen without jumping in to fix or interpret. Hard as it may be to keep from taking your loved one's emotions personally, try. If you find yourself the target of anger or frustration, remind yourself that anger is often a defense against fear and terror. Bear witness to that, too, as you keep breathing.

Work to distinguish your loved one's feelings from your own. It's important to realize that dying is not a horror for everybody. There is such a thing as an appropriate death, a death that has been accepted by the person who's facing it. Your fears aren't universal, and it's important not to assume that the turmoil inside you belongs to the person in the bed.

Whatever comes up, do your best to simply listen. You'll have your chance to speak soon enough. If you stop loved ones from talking because they're upset, or because they're upsetting you, they're likely to retreat from self-disclosure and honesty and lose the opportunity for healing that can come from expressing what matters to them.

Use your breath as a tether. If you find that you're lost in your own reactions, or that the drunken monkey has taken you out for another wild ride, be easy on yourself. Take a few slow breaths to help clear your mind and bring your focus back to the other person. Inside the breath is a center point of pure receiving where you can relax your opinions and assumptions and make room for the possibility of hearing something new in the other person's stories—or letting those stories rest in an embracing silence. When there is only silence, let that be enough.

Stay with Whatever Comes Up

Your heart-centered listening creates an accepting space in which the other person can feel safe enough to express him- or herself fully. I learned much about that from Shanti volunteers, who repeatedly showed me the power of keeping an intent focus on the other person's words, silences, and nonverbal cues while listening with one's own intuition, open to receiving whatever comes.

"I used to like to hear the sound of my own voice and how I was trying to be helpful," says a former volunteer named Danny Castelow, who now works with the San Francisco AIDS Foundation. "But I learned that being quiet and allowing the other person to do most of the talking was the thing that was helpful. No advice, no solutions, no interrupting. I've learned to shut off my mind, unlike my earlier talkative self. And when I do, it's amazing how often people learn to solve their own problems or come up with an insight that's important to them."

He reflected on a story he'd told me years ago for my book *Sometimes My Heart Goes Numb,* which discusses caregiving during the AIDS crisis of the 1980s and 1990s. He still thinks about a client from that time who had sixteen different infections and began one of their visits by listing them all.

"I was tired, overworked, and really wanted to cut him off, to stop the flow of words," Danny says. "But his diction was so perfect, like he was an actor, and something inside me told me to listen and wait for him to finish: 'I have Kaposi's sarcoma, and cytomegalovirus, and . . .' I realized afterward that he was talking about some of the most central things in his life, and he wanted an audience for his recitation. He really wanted to tell me all the things that were afflicting him. So, I sat still and simply listened until he finished.

"He blew my mind when he got to the end. That's when he said, 'Despite everything that's going wrong with my body, I'm having a good life.' He came to that conclusion himself, and it was necessary for him to tell me his list of infections before he could get there.

"If I had interrupted him, and he hadn't had a chance to recite his list, he might never have concluded that he was having a good life, that he was, in some deep way, still himself, still okay. If I had stopped the flow of his words, if I had rushed him along and not allowed him adequate time, his wonderful conclusion that he was living a good life might never have been spoken and understood. He was one of the first people to teach me the importance of listening from the heart, really listening deeply to what's being said—and not said—by the people I care for."

Danny added, "Now I'm comfortable with silence. I can sit still without saying anything for long minutes at a time. Since I'm not a clinician, and I'm not diagnosing anyone or assessing them like a professional, they feel freer to tell me things, to tell me what's on their mind. They seem to trust me more when I shut my mouth and listen. I don't give them advice. Mostly I listen to what they have to say. I have more time than the professionals do to really listen, to allow more time for discussion. That's also what encourages them to dig deeper into what's on their mind. Things surface when I sit quietly and allow people to share, and when I value what they say."

Let the Other Person Lead

Sitting with your friend or family member, quietly paying attention, is all you need to do. When the other person is speaking, forget trying to have a productive conversation—or any other goal—and let him or her take the lead. You may have all sorts of thoughts about what your loved one *should* be saying, but quiet your mind so you hear what's actually being said. You're not there to steer things in a particular direction, even when you are positive it would be best to zero in on topic X or Y instead of wasting time with small talk. You don't know what your loved one wants, or why. Maybe the other person is talking about sports or what's on TV because what she craves most in that moment is relief from the intense conversations she's been having with other family members or her doctors and nurses.

I was certain that I was doing what was best for my father during the weeks right after his diagnosis—when I kept myself too busy "helping him" to visit more than a few minutes. However, I was actually focused on what felt best to *me*. So, it's with great compassion that I say this: the more strongly you feel compelled to save your loved one, rather than doing the hard work of listening from the heart, the more you may be satisfying your own needs, and not theirs. Gently notice that and try once more to listen from the heart.

Your mind may tell you that there's nothing new in what your loved one is saying; it would be so much better to use your remaining time together to talk about something besides a meaningless reprise of complaints or facts you've heard a million times. But, listening from the heart includes receiving the familiar, annoying, and "time-wasting" elements, too, and experiencing what they hold today.

During my father's dying time, he often complained that my mother was driving him crazy—she was alternately distraught over his pain and upset when he asked her to keep him company. It was extremely tempting to play peacemaker or relationship therapist, roles so many adult children slip into. But, I held back words such as "Why don't you get clear on precisely what you want from her and communicate it ASAP? This situation must be terribly hard for her too."

It wasn't easy to keep from summarizing my father's comments "so he could hear what he sounded like" or to resist offering to speak with my mother about "their situation." Harder yet was quieting the chatter in my mind about how I'd been listening to these same complaints for years. As Dad talked, I'd sometimes imagine calling my brother and venting to him about how our parents were still going at it, even in the hospital. In time, I got better at bringing myself back to the moment, and I took a deep breath to refocus when I noticed that I was lost in judgments, mental rebuttals, or fears that Mom would intrude on our private conversation.

One evening, Dad talked for thirty minutes about his familiar struggle with Mom and complained again about how he had to "juggle this awful disease with having to tread on pins and needles around your mother." Then, he paused and looked at me with a strange smile.

"You know," he said, "I love that woman to death. Without her, I'd still be Eddie from Brooklyn. She showed me culture, classical music, the arts. We traveled parts of the world together. Most of all, she was central in bringing up you and your brother. Promise me that you'll take care of her after I'm gone," he said.

I told him I would.

You can't know what your loved one longs to say or what depths of feeling might sit just below words that feel overly familiar and even empty to you. By listening from the heart, without expectation, you create an atmosphere that welcomes anything that comes.

With respectful silence, eye contact, and attention—instead of a running commentary—you can make the other person feel like an honored guest and convey that you care about what he or she is sharing with you. Sometimes the dying want to protect us from the fears, concerns, regrets, or unresolved feelings from the past that they most need to talk about. It happens for many reasons: they're embarrassed, they don't want to burden or upset us, or they don't think talking will do any good. But when we keep listening, we communicate that we're not going anywhere, no matter what. It's the most powerful proof we can give that we can handle their truth.

Sometimes the truth will be that they're in pain, in turmoil, or in despair. Sometimes what they want will be the opposite of what you'd want for yourself. All of this can test your emotional and psychological resources, and it can be challenging to unplug your automatic reactions. After all, most of us are not Zen monks, and, whether monks or not, our relationships are often complex. The person who's dying may well be someone with whom you have issues—a difficult parent, a friend or ex who hurt you and whom you haven't completely forgiven, or a loved one you hurt. Jealousy, guilt, and resentments don't disappear because someone is dying. But, healing can come as you quiet yourself and listen. When old emotions rise, remind yourself that you have a chance to change the tone of the relationship from anger, incompleteness, or animosity to something closer to love, affection, and caring.

Remember, too, that the potential for growth may be greater at the end of life than at any other time. The dying person has the capacity to change dramatically—and one of the things that can facilitate the shift is your willingness to listen from the heart. When you can put aside old assumptions as you listen to stories you thought you knew, you may discover something of yourself in him or her and see your loved one with new empathy—making it possible for both of you to step out of old roles.

A Presence That Says, "I'm Here"

I know "listen from the heart" may sound like a platitude you've heard 10,000 times, but my decades of caring for the dying have shown me the healing power locked into those familiar words. There's much more to listening than smiling and nodding your head. It's a practice of deep presence, and, in time, you won't just hear the other person's words. You'll be able to sense his or her experience in your body and learn from what you feel.

This kind of mindfulness makes it possible to surrender your own agenda and any game plan for what you'll do. You don't have to *do* anything. I sat many times with my mother as she was dying, and when she was quiet I'd put my hand on hers or just sit beside her. Sometimes, after twenty or thirty minutes of silence, she'd say, "I'm so glad you're here." More than any cure I tried to find or gift I brought, what she valued most was having someone who was willing to share her situation—by being there, witnessing both her words and her silences.

The effects of receiving heart-deep listening can be singularly healing. Some people have never been genuinely listened to in their lives, and many have told me that experiencing it gave them a new kind of hope, dignity, and self-worth. You can offer all that to your loved ones by receiving their stories, their fears, and their wisdom.

Early on as a psychologist at CRI, where I spent years learning what brings the most comfort to people with terminal conditions, I sat with Sam, a fifty-five-year-old truck driver with advanced lymphosarcoma. Sam had story after story about driving a big rig, often late at night, across the country. It was lonely on the open road, he said, and so dark. Out there, he lived with the constant fear that his gas would run out and he might not make it to the next stop. Truckers, he told me, hunger for human contact. He always missed his family.

He often shared his stark and sometimes harrowing tales of the road for thirty minutes. Then, looking me squarely in the eye, he would say, "I hope you realize I'm not just talkin' about trucks."

That led us to the fears he faced now. His pain was increasing. He was losing weight. And, visitors were few in this "pretty scary place." I did what I could—alerting his nurses to the pain, and listening. Always listening. I wasn't sure I was making any difference at all, but he told a nurse after one of our visits that things were "easier now that I can speak my mind."

It may feel to you as though you're not doing anything when you're letting loved ones talk about the fear, the pain, and everything else that's part of their life now. But in your willingness to be touched by what they offer you, you're saying that they matter to you, that their stories have meaning, their lives have meaning, and your relationship has meaning.

Every time you listen from the heart, you tell your loved one, "I'm here. We're still in this life side by side, and I'm not scared off. We're in it to the end, connected. I care what you have to say, and I'm absorbing it as completely as I can."

If you can do only one thing for your loved one, listen from the heart.

Chapter Two
I Will Speak from the Heart

THE 2ND COMMITMENT
I will speak to you kindly, truthfully,
and openly, pushing aside my need to advise
or to protect you by lying. I will give you
the best of myself, as best I can.

Your mind can spin with all there is to absorb and feel at the bedside of your loved one. With so much going on inside, it's hard to know what to say, and many people feel paralyzed with worry about how to say the right thing, by which they mean anything that won't inadvertently hurt the other person or reopen an old wound.

In truth, there are no perfect words, but there is a way of speaking—speaking from the heart—that can become a vehicle and a filter for what you want to express. Speaking from the heart involves being truthful, kind, and open, always with the goal of drawing closer to the other person and sharing what both of you are experiencing.

Much of this kind of speaking involves encouraging the *other* person to talk openly about what he or she is thinking and feeling. You can do this by both asking questions and expressing what you feel, not what you *think* you ought to be feeling, even when your emotions are complicated or confused.

When you speak with care, loving kindness, and honesty, the other person can trust that you are being authentic, and that you mean what you say. That frees him or her to respond in kind.

Like listening from the heart, this kind of speaking is grounded in the present as well as in your body and breath. It's important to stay in the here and now and not drift to fears about the future or impressions from the past. Allow what you say to flow from what's going on in the room, both inside and outside yourself.

Don't worry about getting every word exactly right. It's easy to be so cautious at first, so engrossed in rehearsing what you want to say, that you feel awkward saying anything at all. But with practice, you'll learn to trust yourself more, and your comments will become less premeditated, more spontaneous, and more filled with the kind of honesty that can open you and your loved one to greater intimacy. No matter how you've communicated with him or her in the past, you have a chance now to let your heart guide you to a stronger connection.

Anytime you visit, remind yourself to speak from the heart:

- What do I most want to say to my loved one that I can convey with kindness and honesty?
- What might we say to one another that needs to be said?

And before you say anything, consider these questions:

- Do I intend to be of service?
- Am I trying to bring more closeness, intimacy, and affection into the relationship with what I'm about to say?

Don't overthink it. Just connect to your heart before you speak.

Talking About the Diagnosis and Outlook

We respond to our loved ones' declining condition in many ways—with disbelief, with grief, with anger and fear. Sometimes there's relief. Sometimes what comes up is an urgent need to escape, complete unfinished business, or make amends.

You'll confront most or all of these responses in yourself and in your dying friend or family member, and though you are powerless to change the diagnosis or the likely outcome, you can bring solace and strength as a companion on the journey through and toward the unknown.

You may wonder if it's *really* okay to talk about the diagnosis and your loved one's condition. Many people worry that they'll hurt the other person and hasten his or her decline if they say a word like "cancer" or talk about what the doctors have said. However, I've found that ambiguity can be more painful than the negative reality of the diagnosis. People with advanced cancer and other serious conditions often feel terrible, and they know something is badly wrong with them. They visit oncologists or specialists in other life-threatening illnesses, and the names of their diseases are on the signs they see, the buildings they visit, and literature they receive.

People also notice the nonverbal cues from loved ones who know the truth—averted eyes, sad looks, hunched shoulders, sighs, and tears. All of this conveys the message that the outlook is not good. So when friends and family lie, or never speak openly about what's going on, dying people often fear that the truth is even worse than they know and fantasize about all manner of terrible things—intractable pain and suffering, for instance—which wouldn't be a concern if they had honest information.

I encourage you to share the truth, rather than avoiding it, and ask questions of your loved one's care team when you're unclear about the prognosis and the likely course of the disease. When test results and specialists called in for second opinions concur that the news is grim, most patients and families want to get an estimate of the time that remains, so they know what they're dealing with. But, many doctors leave their answers vague because it's so hard to be precise. In that case, you'll need to be assertive. You can say something such as "It would be very helpful if you could give us an estimate of the amount of time my loved one has left. We understand that it's an estimate, and things can change, but we'd like to know your educated guess."

The thing to understand is that a prognosis *is* an educated guess, and there are often exceptions and surprises. People may live longer—or for a much shorter time—than anyone's best estimate. What we know for certain is that in this final phase of life, no matter how long it lasts, truth and kindness are of the highest value. Your loved one will let you know what he or she is ready to hear and say by engaging in the topic with you, changing the subject, staying silent, or even saying, "I'd rather not talk about it now." Do your best to honor that.

How to Help Your Loved One Understand the Bad News

My brother Jon and I were at the hospital with my parents when my father's doctor broke the news that Dad's liver cancer was advanced, spreading, and untreatable. Dad began to cry—the first time I'd ever seen him in tears—and he haltingly asked Jon and me to leave the room while he and Mom got the details. In part, I think, he was embarrassed and ashamed to be crying in front of us. And, he probably wanted to shield us from the news, though of course there was no way to do that.

By the time he and my mom emerged from the doctor's office, he was composed and smiling. "Let's get some breakfast," he said, as though nothing had happened. The disconnect was jarring.

When I visited him two days later, I wondered how much he'd actually taken in from the doctor's meeting. Mom had told me that "the doctor gave your father three to six months at most," and Dad seemed too happy for a guy who had just learned he had so little time left.

"How are you feeling about what the doctor said?" I asked him.

At first, he tried to put a positive spin on everything. "You never know how things will turn out," he said. Such words are often people's way of keeping themselves, and loved ones, from drowning in the sadness that comes with a dire prognosis.

But when you signal your openness to the other person's reality and share your own feelings, you often clear the way for him or her to express more vulnerability. "I'm willing to talk about anything that's on your mind, Dad," I told him, "and if I cry or if you do, it's because we love each other."

Finally, he asked me, "How do you think things will play out for me, Son?"

"I'm not sure, Dad," I said. "I know the liver cancer is serious, but I also know that hospice is very good at treating pain and making people in exactly your situation comfortable. I'd like to stay closely involved in your care as part of the team. Is that okay?"

Dad beamed and replied, "It's more than okay. I'd really appreciate that a lot. After all, between you and me, all those people in white coats give me the creeps. I haven't gotten much good news from them lately."

That opening let us begin to talk about specifics. I asked what the doctor had told him about the prognosis and whether he was in pain. His most pressing concern was what would happen if the pain increased, and I told him that we could ask his hospice nurse to intervene immediately anytime he needed relief.

We talked later about how he'd like to spend his remaining time. It can feel strange to acknowledge the reality that comes with the words, "What would you like to do in the time you have left?" However, asking lets you know, instead of guess, what the other person really wants. Some want to travel to see beloved places or people; others have projects in mind to complete while they still have the strength. My father's desires were simple. He wanted to watch old movies with Mom, Jon, and me; go anywhere he could to "see natural beauty"; and teach his class on "telling a good joke" at the North Berkeley Senior Center for as long as his energy permitted.

We made it a priority to do all those things.

Understanding Comes in Stages

If you're with a loved one soon after the diagnosis and prognosis, ask questions to find out what he or she understands about how much time remains, how his or her condition will progress, what effects that will have, and how pain and other needs for care will be managed. Keep in mind that important information often has to be gently repeated over many days, or even weeks, before your loved one fully comprehends it.

I was reminded of this when I met a CEO who had been diagnosed with seriously advanced bone cancer. He was a take-charge guy, used to orchestrating meetings and absorbing facts, but when I asked him if he was clear about his condition—the prognosis, the kind of pain he might experience, and so on—he said flatly, "I have no idea what to expect." His chart indicated that his doctor had explained everything to him, but, clearly, the information hadn't penetrated. I suggested that we meet again with his care team, and he asked for time to make a list of questions beforehand. Preparing in that way let him feel more in control, less ambushed by information he needed to absorb.

No matter who we are, the words "I'm dying" reverberate so loudly in our mind that, for a while, they drown out everything else. We have to accept that inescapable fact before being able to focus on hows and whys and details. And, acceptance takes time. Expect that it may come slowly for your loved one.

Speaking from the Heart About Bad News
SEVEN GUIDELINES

Because the first conversations are so difficult for everyone, I've developed a set of guidelines to help friends and family members speak from the heart while discussing bad news. The goal of conversations just after a doctor has shared the diagnosis and prognosis is to find out what your loved one understands and to share your understanding of what the news means. More than that, you'll want to get a sense of how the other person feels about it and discover what he or she wants most during this final period of life.

The following seven items, based on compassion and common sense, will help you set the best possible stage for that discussion, even as you're processing your own feelings. Shanti volunteers have used them for many years.

1. Have the conversation in a comfortable place where you're not likely to be interrupted.

2. Before you begin, take a deep breath. Empathize with your loved one by asking yourself, "If it were my diagnosis and prognosis, what would this new information mean to me?"

3. Ask questions instead of pontificating about the facts, or what your Internet searches have turned up. You're all trying to accept this new reality, and each person will do it in a different way. Start with questions such as "What did the doctor tell you in that meeting the other day?"

4. Don't try to discuss everything that's on your mind with your loved one, only the most important things. Everyone can easily be overwhelmed by what's going on, so aim to keep questions and suggestions bite-size. Rather than saying, "Tell me everything your doc told you," it's better to ask, "What do you remember from the talk with your doctor?" Instead of saying, "I'll let everyone important to you know what's going on, so they can visit," ask, "Who would you like me to tell about what's going on with you?"

5. Simplicity is a virtue. If you can't say or explain something simply, you'll probably end up confusing things. Remember that one of the best kinds of expertise you can develop right now is the ability to ask questions. It's more helpful to say,

"Would you like me to find someone who can give us a second opinion?" than to jump in and research every expert on the disease.

6. Give the other person time to respond, ask questions, or express emotion.

7. Don't try to confront denial with the truth and insist that your loved one immediately accept his or her new reality. People have the right to take in the truth at their own rate.

At Shanti, we work to accept whatever a person believes is true for him or her, to honor that truth, and to sit with it, just as the person has to. The subtext is always "No matter what, I'm on your side, pulling for you." This is an attitude that will serve both of you well throughout the dying time.

Hope and Positivity

Hope is a powerful force, and in talking about a person's prognosis, I've always advised being realistic without slamming the door on the possibility that things will improve. You can be gentle with the truth by saying things such as

"You've got a serious illness/situation, and the docs say you've got [this much time] left, but occasionally some people get past conditions like this, or they live longer than anyone expects. I wish I could say that things are looking positive; however, I can't. But I'm prepared to be surprised."

Miracles *are* possible, but we consider them to be miraculous precisely because they are so unlikely, so rare. When the experts and your own eyes tell you that your loved one's body is failing, the hope for a miracle recovery fades. But, you and your loved one can continue to hope for other things and draw on the kind of hope that has brought many people the strength to complete their lives in a way that gives them peace.

Your loved one may be sustained by the hope of going home to die, the desire to see a new grandchild, the need to finish a project, or the act of passing on the wisdom he or she values most. People often have hopes of reconciling with someone, unburdening themselves of an old secret or guilt, forgiving, or being forgiven. *These* are the hopes it's so important to talk about and help your loved one act on.

Some people believe that our words and thoughts create reality, and if we can manage to have only positive thoughts and speak only positive words, the dying person won't die. This can play out as pressure not to talk about anything negative with a dying loved one, as if anything that's not cheerful and uplifting will only hasten death.

The dying can wind up trapped in a place where it's taboo to discuss some of their consuming thoughts and feelings about pain, dying, and loss or make plans for their final days. It feels cruel to me to effectively say to them that if they talk about what they're going through, they aren't rooting for a cure, or that they're not trying hard enough to stay alive. Even the most positive people want to talk about their fears and anxieties and concerns, especially at the end of life. And, they can feel terribly abandoned when they don't have a chance to do that.

Danny Castelow, a Shanti volunteer I mentioned earlier, remembers dropping in to see his client Joe and finding a birthday party in progress. "I knew that Joe had just been told by his doctor that he was being transferred to hospice care because of the severity of his illness. He was destroyed by the news, but no one else in the room knew about his transfer. Everyone was so invested in the party, in trying to make him feel better, that they never took the time to really talk to him, to listen to how he was really doing. The guy couldn't care less about his birthday. He was devastated.

"I stayed for a while, smiled a little at Joe, and made eye contact with him. When I asked him how he was doing, he said he was fine. But, I saw a small tear collecting in the corner of his eye. 'I'll come and visit you again later,' I said. When I returned a few hours later and mentioned what I'd noticed, he began to bawl. The dam broke, and he just sobbed without saying a word. I think it was therapeutic for him to be able to cry with big body heaves. After he stopped, we talked about hospice, what to expect, and how people would be caring for him who really knew how to handle the challenges he was facing. Because I spoke from the heart about what I was seeing, because I didn't ignore what was happening, he was able to also speak from the heart. My truth telling allowed him to speak his truths."

Joe was amazed. "You were really listening to me," he told Danny. "And when you said something, it was clear that you were speaking honestly. So many other people around me are afraid of my situation and want to put their own positive spin on what's happening and what to say to me. You don't do that. I can trust you to tell me the truth."

"With Joe and many others," Danny explained, "I felt like I did very little except listen intently and speak when something surfaced that wanted to be said. It's not about listening combined with your own thoughts. I try to shut off my mind and listen with my heart, with my body, with my feelings. And sometimes, something surfaces that wants to be said, and it's a game changer, something that's transformative, something that's bigger than anything either of us has known before. It's like when Joe said in our conversation, 'Everything I'm experiencing, I brought on myself. And if I can make the bad things happen, I can find solutions to them.' All I did was nod my head yes and give him a big hug."

People don't go into cardiac arrest when you speak from the heart and tell them the truth of what you see; they make space for the insights that can come. But, you have to learn that. You have to *practice* acknowledging the truth. It's easier to do what Joe's family and friends did: carry on as if death isn't in the room with you.

So much is going on inside your loved one—hopes, regrets, love, confusion, and despair. Being willing to talk about all of that won't change the outcome, but you can make the ongoing experience much less difficult and lonely if you are willing to share it.

Conversations That Keep You Connected

If you're visiting a dying friend or relative you haven't seen in a while, sometimes reconnecting under these circumstances feels painfully awkward. Be sure to take a moment to center yourself before entering the room. I've always tried to be as natural as possible, frequently smiling a bit when I first see the person. I want to show that I'm not afraid of the situation, that things can be somewhat normal despite the diagnosis.

I know it sounds obvious, but the talks you have now can be as ordinary as any of the many others you've had with your loved one, which can be easy to forget when both of you are grappling with the news. A conversation might start as follows: "Hi, George. I'm glad to visit. It'll be good to spend some time together. I heard about your diagnosis and wanted to see you. How are you doing today? Do you need anything?"

There's nothing particularly remarkable about that—you know how to do it. One thing I'd stress now, though, is using the skill of listening from the heart to really hear what the other person is saying each time you ask a question. Keep returning to the person's eyes if you get distracted by what's going on in the room, or by the thoughts swirling inside you.

It helps to ask open-ended questions that give the other person the space to process his or her feelings. Rather than setting up a terse yes or no, you can draw the person out by saying, "What was it like to hear your doctor's news?" as opposed to "Were you upset?" Then listen with your heart to the answer.

Find out what the other person can handle today. It helps to say things such as "Is it okay to talk about what the next steps are, or would you rather talk about something else? We can talk about whatever you have on your mind. I'm here for you no matter what." If you're the person who's always talked sports or politics with your loved one, it may well be that the other person will want to segue into that territory. That's fine—it can be a welcome relief to think about "normal" life. But, don't be afraid to talk about what you're feeling. Speaking from the heart means expressing your genuine feelings and allowing yourself to say things such as "I'm so sorry this is happening," and "This totally sucks," as well as "I love you," which may not have been part of your friend or office vocabulary.

If you get tangled in thoughts and difficult emotions because of what you see or hear, remind yourself that asking questions will always help you shift your attention to your loved one, instead of your own turmoil. When you can, take the risk of going deeper. Although it may be a challenge emotionally for both of you, it's often important to ask, "What are you really feeling about what's happening to you?" The responses you hear each time you ask this question—assuming the other person is willing to discuss his or her feelings with you—can lead you to truthful conversation and give both of you a greater sense of peace.

You may think offering to have such an intimate conversation with someone you may not know very well—an acquaintance or a casual friend—isn't appropriate. But if you are moved to offer, I encourage you to do so. I've noticed that it's sometimes the people who haven't been particularly close who become the most important and least emotionally upset members of the dying person's circle. You may turn out to be the person who's most willing to delve into tough issues if you show that you are open to it.

Timing is everything in such conversations. Sometimes your loved one will be too sad to have a "serious" conversation or simply won't want to engage. I've found, however, that a question may percolate in a person's mind and heart and come up again in a thoughtful moment later. Stay receptive by continuing to speak and listen from the heart.

Remember That You're Not the Expert

The dying time is full of questions with no complete or satisfactory answers that can come from you. Your loved one may ask you, "What will happen next with my disease?" or "Is there an afterlife?" or "Did my life mean anything?"

It helps a great deal to get comfortable with not knowing, and not *having* to know, the answers. On the cancer ward, if someone asked, "What's going to happen to me?" I would reach for responses that would help us talk things through and find our way together. I might say something such as "I just have some guesses, but my assumption is that you know more about what's going on than I do. You're living it. So, why don't we talk? I'll give you my impression, and you give me yours, and we'll be honest with each other." If someone asked, "Why is this happening?" I learned to say, "I wish I knew. It's not fair."

A lot of us are problem solvers accustomed to analyzing situations, categorizing what's going on, and coming up with solutions. However, there's no fix, no cure, for the problem of dying. It's helpful to remember that the only expert on what's happening within a person during the dying time is that person. It can't be you.

Even if you *are* a psychotherapist or counselor, it's important not to act like one with a dying loved one by analyzing or interpreting what he or she says. If your loved one tells you something such as "My doc doesn't care at all about me. I haven't seen him in days," you may be tempted to respond by saying, "What you really meant to say is that he's really busy and only comes when he has something to tell you," or "I'm sure he cares, he's just busy."

Such statements tend to place you in a superior position and violate the mutuality of your relationship. Interpreting your loved one's words can feel infuriating and distancing to him or her. It's more helpful to ask what you can do to help: "Would it be useful for me to try to get the doc in here to have a conversation with you?" I've often been surprised at how frequently the other person says, "No, I don't really need to see him."

Try to steer away from comments that include the words "what you really mean is" or "what I think you're trying to say is" or "that story is *really* about [your childhood/your mother/your career], isn't it?" They're tip-offs to your loved one that you are filtering things largely through your own reality, and he or she may shut down and stop trying to communicate and connect with you.

You may feel compelled to weigh in about what would be best for your loved one or offer your take on what he or she needs, but this, too, creates distance by suggesting that you have some special expertise or knowledge that the other person doesn't have. Repeatedly giving advice can convey a certain arrogance—the opposite of the humility that's so vital in close relationships.

So keep asking questions instead of making assumptions. For instance, if something your loved one says leads you to believe that he or she might have an interest in a particular topic, say, spirituality, steer away from advice such as "You'll find a lot of answers in this new book on Buddhism." First find out if your impressions were correct by *asking,* "Are you interested in reading about the Dalai Lama?" When you do this, the thoughts you offer feel more like a gift than another prescription from another expert.

If your loved one asks you directly, "What should I do?" you don't need to shut him or her out by saying, "I don't give advice." It's most helpful to use words such as "If it were me, my guess is that I would [do this]." That lets you share your thoughts without imposing them on the other person.

Danny Castelow talked about how he does this: "I feel like the doorman to people's problems by offering ideas. But, the decision about solutions is theirs alone. They have to walk through the door. If they ask me what I would do in their situation, I'll speak from the heart and tell them as best I can. But, they're the ones who make the eventual decision. My intention is to bring people some peace, to help reduce their anxiety.

"I have a Native American friend who, when I share with him any problem I'm struggling with, pauses and then says, 'Call your spirit back,'" Danny adds. "What he means is that when you connect with your spirit, when you reclaim your power, you'll know what to do. He's right. I've discovered that people, especially when they're scared, give away their power, their spirit, and feel helpless. And, they don't need to. When I listen and then speak from the heart, it seems to empower people, to encourage them to move more confidently toward a solution to their problems. I help them call their spirit back."

When Anger and Resentment Are Getting in the Way

You may have had a difficult history with the person who's dying—it's fairly common for family members to be caring for someone who has abused, neglected, or mistreated them, or broken their trust. And if that's the case, you may come into this dying time full of anger, resentments, and lingering pain.

That was true for the family of a jazz musician I met on the cancer ward. Don was a talented pianist who had spent his life in smoky clubs, devoted to his music. In all his years of performing, he'd rarely been without a cigarette and a stiff drink when he sat down at the keyboard. Don's wife Jean, a medical social worker, worried over his health, and when he developed a cough and began to lose weight, she and their kids begged him to at least cut back on the smoking. But music, he made clear, was "the most important thing in my life," and cigarettes were part of it.

When Don was diagnosed with late-stage lung cancer, his family was bitter and resentful. They were scared and sad, but, mostly, they were furious because he'd "brought his cancer on himself" and he'd always made them second to his music. It was impossible for them to visit without being overtaken by blame, judgment, and what felt like years of frustration, disappointment, and anger.

The past doesn't go away just because someone is dying. But, there *is* a chance in the present to create a more fulfilling end to the story—if you are willing to work through the emotions that are coming between you and the complex, difficult person you are losing.

If you're extremely upset, don't visit until you vent your feelings in private with a counselor or write a letter that describes your fury and its reasons—a letter that you don't send or share. I highly recommend talking to a social worker, spiritual counselor, or psychologist on the hospital staff or hospice team who can help you release your volatile emotions and focus on the words and actions that will be most healing to all of you.

Don's family yelled, seethed, and cried as they talked about him and the way he was abandoning them. They were incredulous and wary when I brought up forgiveness: "*Forgive* him? You're out of your mind." But as we talked through what forgiveness really means, it was a choice that made sense to them.

Forgiveness doesn't mean sucking it up and pretending the other person didn't wrong you or cause you terrible pain. It doesn't require forgetting what happened, admitting you were wrong, or waiting for the other person to apologize. It doesn't even have to involve telling the other person you've forgiven him or her.

Instead, forgiveness involves setting down the burden that comes with keeping your resentment and rage alive in the present. In forgiving someone, you acknowledge your own pain and find ways to move beyond it without changing the past or the other person. Some people do this by saying, "These feelings are hurting me. I'm going to let them go." You don't have to forgive; however, after you allow yourself to express your anger fully in the presence of a counselor, you may decide you want to.

I went with Don's family when they felt they were ready to visit with him. Because of the work we'd done on anger and forgiveness, all the family members were able to speak from the heart more easily. I encouraged them to talk with Don about the good times they'd enjoyed—including the wonderful music that he'd given to them and his audiences— and to feel their love for him.

Speaking from the Heart About a Painful Past

As you allow love to surface at the end of your loved one's life, the tougher stuff won't automatically disappear, and I told Don's family that they didn't have to steer clear of talking about their history with him. But, it was important to keep the principles of speaking from the heart in mind. Speaking from the heart, at its core, is about serving the other person.

While you may hope to have a chance to settle scores, speak up for yourself, and, perhaps, finally get an apology that you've been waiting on for a lifetime, that won't automatically happen. My best counsel is to speak your truth and accept that while you can create an opening for the other person to discuss the past with you, you can't create a particular outcome. Many people, reviewing their lives in the dying time, want to apologize and ask for forgiveness. But many don't, or can't. Keeping expectations in check is vital.

Stay open. Keep in mind that you are here, caring for your loved one, because of the person *you* are and because of the compassion you have allowed yourself to feel for the flawed, suffering human in front of you. It's helpful, realistic, and healing to say something such as "We've got some really rough stuff in our history, and I want to see if we can get past it during this difficult time. I'm happy to talk about any of it you want to, but if you don't, I understand."

The goal of talking about old pain is to create closeness, not get a conviction. If your loved one is in a receptive mood, you might bring up a difficult episode with words such as "Dad, your job kept you so busy that you were never around when I was growing up. It made me sad and upset and sometimes angry when you weren't there. I never quite understood it because I wanted my father around. What was going on for you at that time?"

By keeping the focus on your own feelings rather than issuing an indictment and asking a question that might give both of you more insight into your history, you can create a point of contact and, perhaps, allow new understanding to emerge. That's always the goal of speaking from the heart—whether you're talking with your loved one about a happy memory or a rough time in your relationship.

Chapter Three
I Will Act from the Heart

THE 3RD COMMITMENT

I will act from the heart, focusing on you and what you need most, rather than on my own desire to keep fixing, moving, or protecting myself with distance. I will do my best to let compassion for you guide my actions.

One of the most difficult challenges you'll face as you spend time with your loved one is coping with the desire to fix the situation and make everything better. The urge to do that when someone is dying is almost primal. However, acting from the heart requires you to still the impulse to fix or help and focus on being of service. The difference may seem to be a matter of semantics, but each of those words—*fix, help,* and *serve*—is rooted in a particular motivation that colors how your loved one experiences what you do and shapes the relationship between you.

What's Wrong with Trying to Fix Things?

Fixing feels completely normal and, often, quite virtuous. All of us want to repair the situation that's causing our loved ones to suffer, and there's no question that if we could cure them, we would. But as I tell my students and volunteers, you fix machines, not people. While you may fantasize about being the person who rides in with a miracle and be consumed by the effort to fix every problem, including your loved one's condition, your solutions may not be what he or she wants. That's the danger of fixing: it's frequently driven by a desire to make *yourself* feel better—less helpless, less sad, more in control of the situation—rather than a real attempt to put the other person first.

I learned this humbling lesson when my father was dying and I researched experimental cures for his liver cancer. As I alluded to in the first chapter, I was positive Dad's doctors had missed something, and there must have been a treatment they hadn't considered. I spent every free hour in the library, and when I excitedly brought back information on a new drug trial my father might be able to enter, he told me he wasn't interested. "I believe my doctors when they tell me what's going on," he said. "There's no cure for me. We both know that."

But, I wasn't ready to accept that. Desperate not to lose him, I surged into cancer-warrior mode, believing that I could help him become a survivor. If only he could shake his resignation, we could beat this thing. I was sure of it. I turned my research efforts to finding out which traits survivors had in common and how they'd cultivated them. I'd never seen my dad as much of a fighter, yet I was determined to make him one.

One evening, I showed up at his house with a documentary featuring interviews of people who'd battled back from terminal diagnoses.

"This is one of the videos I've mentioned, Dad. Let's take a look, okay?" I said. "Then we can talk."

I pushed play and settled into the recliner next to his. Just as the title appeared, he got up to go to the john. Given his medications and enlarged prostate, I should have expected it.

I paused the tape and then adjusted the window blinds, poured him a glass of water, and waited. He returned after a long interval.

"So, good buddy," he said vaguely, "where were we?"

"The videos, Dad."

Once more I pressed play. On the screen, a parade of older men and women told inspirational stories about surviving after being diagnosed with terminal illnesses. These were "exceptional patients," so termed by the physician who introduced them. I especially wanted Dad to hear the man who spoke of "fighting for my life against the so-called logic of the situation facing me." I liked that phrase: *the so-called logic of the situation*. It encouraged me to dismiss any so-called prognosis that said my father would be gone in a few months. Dad could do that too.

I looked over at him as the survivors continued to talk about the importance of a positive outlook, proper diet, exercise, and relaxation as complements to traditional therapies.

"Dad, this is what I've been talking about . . ." I stopped speaking when I saw his eyes were closed. He was snoring softly.

I slammed down the lever of my recliner, and the chair shot upright with a bang. Startled, Dad rubbed his eyes. I started the video over, and, again, he fell asleep.

When I started it a third time, he stopped me.

"Those videos . . . what they're saying," he said slowly, "it's just not me." His smile was apologetic.

"How is it *not you*?" I demanded.

"My first doc, that cancer specialist, told me there was nothing he could do," he said. "And then, after that, the latest one said I didn't qualify for that new freezing treatment."

"The cryosurgery, you mean."

"Yes, that's it. He said I didn't qualify." Dad was not smiling now. He looked as sad as I was desperate. "Look, I know I have a lot to live for." His tone was defensive. "Everyone— you and your brother, your mother, friends at the senior center—everybody keeps saying it." He balled his hands into fists. "I understand, okay? I get it. I'm supposed to fight for my life."

Dad stared at the TV, his expression as blank as the screen. The words he didn't say hung between us: *Your way isn't for me. I know I'm dying. Please let me go.*

We sat and watched the shadows move across the wall in the late afternoon, and something began to unclench in me—the need for Dad to be different, for everything to be different. At last, I let myself *be* with him, simply present, simply listening. We were together now, and that was what mattered—not my videos and plans and the constant motion I used to run from the reality that had wrapped itself around us.

"Charlie, I love you," he said quietly. And in that moment, I finally understood how much I needed to turn from my own agendas and be there emotionally for him. Perhaps no cure would come, but there would be healing. Death might end his life but never our relationship.

"I love you too," I told him.

We hugged each other tightly, silently expressing all that needed to be said.

The rest of our time together—another several months—connected us in a new way. Without my agenda and all my crazed activity, I was less armored, more available to him; we could face the end as equals, as father and son.

Like many people I'd seen through the years, I had assumed I knew what my father needed and expected that the next steps I saw for him would naturally be what he wanted. As I rushed to fix things, I never thought to ask. Maybe that's because everything I was doing felt right to me. I was used to seeing what needed to be done and stepping in to do it. My head knew exactly what to do and how to make a plan. However, in all my expert fixing, I forgot to engage my heart and make an emotional connection with my father.

As I look back, I notice how much I wanted to be a hero, so both of us could somehow rise above the pain. What healed both of us, though, was facing the truth—Dad's truth—and that allowed us to be with each other. Our emotional connection, I know now, was everything.

The Drawbacks of Helping

Helping is a close cousin of fixing, though it seems entirely positive and focused on the other person. What could be the problem with helping someone at a time of great need? Sometimes there seems to be so much to do, so many needs to meet, that it can be hard to know where to start. How could you *not* help? So, you do your best, hoping that it will be enough.

It's surprisingly easy to help a person efficiently yet forget to slow down long enough to be with them emotionally. I noticed this often on the cancer ward, where patients complained about doctors and nurses who came in, took vitals, or offered meds and then made a quick U-turn at the foot of the bed instead of pausing to look into their eyes or say a kind word.

Like some of those stressed professionals, you may bring your loved ones your efficiency, your energy, and your executive sense of what needs to be done and how best to do it. You may step in to wash dishes or cook for the caregivers, change soiled laundry, care for pets, or pay bills.

All of this reflects your love, yet such actions may not feel loving to the person in the bed if you stay locked in your head, forgetting—or protecting—your heart. Unintentionally and unknowingly, you may communicate the message, "I'm strong and knowledgeable and well-intentioned and I'll take care of things." But, that's different from "I'm with you. I love you. I know you're more than the disease. How are you?"

Pouring yourself into helping the other person can give you the sense of being more in control of the situation, but, paradoxically, you may wind up feeling that you can never do enough—because no amount of intervention from you will give you control over your loved one's final stage of life.

At the same time, all your helping can leave your loved one feeling obligated, instead of comforted, and isolated from you rather than relieved by your presence. But, there's a way of addressing your loved one's needs that can help you steer clear of the pitfalls and burdens brought by fixing and helping: adopting an attitude of service.

You Are in a Unique Position to Serve

Acting from the heart requires us to be *with* our loved ones during the dying time rather than just being *at* the dying time. It also means staying aware of our own feelings of helplessness and noticing the way we might compensate for them with distance, rescue fantasies, or control-freak tendencies.

There's a sense of equality in serving someone, a sense that you are doing for him or her what he or she would do for you were your positions changed. You can best serve your loved one by letting yourself be a fellow human in a vulnerable body. Not a superhero, not a rescuer, but an equal—a human with fears, flaws, and uncertainties who is learning about dying side by side with the other person and accompanying him or her through the experience.

Focusing on service bridges the gap between you and your friend or family member by reminding you to always think about the person and his or her needs and preferences above all else. It's a human, heart-based approach, not a mechanistic, problem-solving one.

You're in a particularly good position to serve your loved one because you know him or her so well. You can still remember and see the *whole* person, someone whose interests and concerns and identity are vaster than the illness, and you can stay connected to your loved one's larger self, the part that endures despite the condition, independent of it. Bharat Lindemood, one of Shanti's exemplary caregivers, described to me how he does that with each person he visits.

"When I look deeply into the eyes of someone who is suffering, I can see that it's my Beloved, the Divine, looking back at me," he said. "It's the Eternal in the other person. I'm trying to connect with the part of the other person that is their soul, the part that's more than physical or mental or emotional. When I do, it gives us both more spaciousness and their tragedy or their challenges become more of an expression of the human predicament, bigger than just their singular, isolating situation. The people I care for are subjects to me, not objects. I can often feel the love in me connecting with their love, a connection formed soul to soul."

You may not think in terms of seeing God in the eyes of your loved one, but you can think of making a connection with the eternal part of that person, or the "light" inside him or her. "When I act from the heart this way," Bharat said, "I'm fully with the other person. It's based primarily on first listening from the heart, listening attentively prior to any action on my part. Listening, especially as a fellow soul, is the deepest way of being with them fully. When I'm interacting with an open heart, I'm relatively undefended, not walling off their experience or my reaction to it or the strong feelings that can come with their pain and suffering."

Bharat emphasized the power of simply witnessing what's happening, something he not only aims to do himself but also encourages in those he cares for. "Sometimes when I'm with someone who is struggling, I say, 'Who you are is not just a personality defect, some flaw. The part of you that's struggling is just part of who you are. We're all also what's greater in us, our souls that witness everything but don't judge or have particular preferences. The part of us that's simply aware of what's going on.' I encourage them to identify with that part, with the witness, to simply observe what's going on without judging it," he said.

"When they do that, they can witness what's going on in their situation emotionally and physically but not be as strongly affected by those aspects of their experience. At times, in a deeper sense, at the level of simply observing, of pure awareness, they're okay, they're safe. They realize that they can't be destroyed by their physical and emotional condition. What surfaces is the self-soothing voice of their soul, like an inner friend, an ally."

Witnessing. Listening. Your unadorned, caring presence and willingness to be with what *is* make it safe for a sense of comfort to emerge, despite all that's happening. You serve your loved one in a profound way when that happens.

Every moment is different, so each time you visit, or come back to the bedside, open yourself to your loved one by listening from the heart and experiencing the person in front of you today. Then ask yourself, "How can I offer what's needed and wanted the most, based on what I've asked and observed?" Let everything you bring be "from the heart."

We Can Only Serve when We're Willing to Touch

The first person who helped me distinguish among fixing, helping, and serving was my friend and colleague Rachel Remen, a psychiatrist and author who has been a patient with Crohn's disease for more than five decades. Rachel has had many surgeries and has experienced all three approaches to caring for people. "Fixing and helping create a distance between people, an experience of difference," she told me. "We cannot serve at a distance. We can only serve that to which we are profoundly connected, that which we are willing to touch."

It's odd to think of not touching our loved ones, yet sometimes we *do* physically recoil from bandages or equipment or a beloved face that is distorted by anger or pain. We can easily lose ourselves in confusion, activity, and fear and, thus, cut ourselves off from "touching" the questions that loom largest for us and for our loved ones. So, acting from the heart requires a constant returning—to our connection with our loved one, to what's happening in the moment, to the clarity that stillness and presence can bring.

I think often of a Shanti volunteer named Josie who asked me how best to help her dying husband: "My husband Alex has been in hospice for three months now, and he seems to be rallying," she said, "choosing to stick around because of all the kindness and attention he's receiving from me, his friends, and the hospice team. The hospice nurse tells me this is a common phenomenon—people, like plants, thrive with attention.

"Should I say something about it to Alex and others, open a discussion, or just let it be? I visit him every day, and it's getting more confusing since it's clear that he's also in more and more pain despite the palliative care he's receiving. I'm at a loss to know what to do—encourage him to stay, do things that will make him comfortable, listen to his stories, or suggest that he let go and leave the pain behind. What do you think?"

Josie's questions had many layers, so I began with the most immediate, which was Alex's pain. Fear of physical suffering can be strong at the end of life, and, fortunately, pain is often effectively managed with drugs that won't dull consciousness. Pain management is always a top priority, and I suggested that Josie alert Alex's hospice team to his increasing pain levels and ask how they could make him more comfortable.

Rather than addressing the specifics of the rest of her list, I suggested that she try seeing what would happen if she put aside *any* lists of things she ought to be doing for Alex and tried sitting quietly with him, letting him set the agenda.

That didn't mean being passive. She could listen and speak from the heart, asking questions and paying attention with every part of herself. Being actively present that way would allow her to act from the heart and serve him in the ways that meant the most to him.

Not long after, I received the following note from Josie.

Dear Charlie,

I followed your suggestion and consulted with the hospice nurse about my husband's pain, and they increased his medications. He's more pain-free now and wants to stick around more than ever. The last few times we were together, I stopped racing around trying to do things for him like some sort of super nurse. I sat near his bed and waited until he asked me for something. Occasionally, I'd say in a loving voice, "Do you need anything? Some water or a little ice cream?"

"Just you," he replied as he took my hand and kissed it.

We both began to cry, and it was as if the dam broke. I bent over and hugged him and we clung to each other for a few minutes. "This is why I don't want to die," Alex said. "Everyone's so good to me, especially you. I've never felt so close to you as I do now, and I don't want to lose that."

I told Alex that I felt the same way and that I wanted him to know that it was a privilege to be his wife and to be with him during this time in our lives. Our conversation was so affectionate and so simple, and so were the things I did for Alex. It was about the love we were giving to one another. I realized that we were part of a long line of husbands and wives, stretching back in history and ahead into the future, who would and will care for one another while one is dying.

You were right, Charlie, about not missing out on this important time because I was running around trying to do all sorts of things for my husband and not paying attention to Alex the person, and to me. I'm not sure how much time we've got left, but I'm not frustrated and confused anymore. We're together for now, and that's all that matters to me and to Alex. If the care he's getting from the hospice team and our friends is also helping to keep him alive, then I'm grateful.

With gratitude,

Josie

P.S. I no longer feel torn between my feelings of helplessness and my desire to control things so Alex gets everything he wants and needs, that old sense of never doing enough. I've learned that my being there with Alex and sharing our suffering and joy are enough. From now on, I'll be slowing down and acting from the heart.

What About All Those Things That Really Do Need to Be Done?

Acting from the heart can take endless forms. Simple, necessary acts, such as bringing food, watering plants, walking pets, or taking care of children, are healing gifts to the other person when we're motivated by compassion, caring, and an intention to be of service. Folding clothes, communicating with doctors and nurses, completing a healthcare proxy or a will, or simply being available as a visitor can similarly be concrete expressions of your devotion to your loved one. It's important to come to even the most seemingly modest task with the intention to serve, bringing your sense of dependability, trustworthiness, relationship, and affection.

It's fine to do something practical, such as doing the laundry when a loved one is asleep, cooking a meal and bringing it over, or asking your loved one what tasks he or she would most like to have done. But know yourself. If you're like I was—a Type-A, get-it-done personality—take care to notice when you go into overdrive. For you, especially, it's vital to spend some time sitting still at the bedside of the person who is dying when he or she would like company. Sitting still and bringing your compassionate presence to the other person is not "wasting time." It's the gift of yourself, an act of love.

When Your Loved One Wants Something You Don't

The actions you're called upon to take at the end of life may feel monumental. There can be options for hope-giving treatments, discussions of how best to let life end, or struggles to resolve long-standing rifts or conflicts.

As you witness or participate in tough conversations and decision-making, it's especially important to remember your intention to serve your loved one. Acting from the heart involves listening to the other person's desires, offering your thoughts (if asked) about what you'd do if you were in his or her place, and digging deep to find out what's behind a request or choice that troubles you. It also means honoring your loved one's wishes as best you can—even when you strongly disagree with him or her.

I was stunned when my mother, who seemed to be handling her dying time with unusual grace, brought up the subject of assisted suicide, and asked if I'd let her choose her time to die and help her leave. I was still thinking about what might be going on for her when I stumbled on the cache of sleeping pills she'd been stockpiling so she could take her own life.

I went to her immediately to tell her what I'd found, and I asked why she'd felt the need to consider suicide rather than living out her days as they came. Then, I asked if she had considered the consequences for me—legally and psychologically—if I helped her carry out her plan. We were both upset, so I suggested that we contemplate for fifteen minutes in different rooms what it would be like for us to end her life that way and then imagine how I'd feel afterward. I wanted us to be centered when we talked rather than filled with anxiety and defensiveness.

When we came together again, the first thing she said was, "I can't do this to you. It's selfish of me to ask you to be involved. But, I got scared when I read that dying might just be fading to black. And, what if the pain gets too bad? That still worries me."

I thanked her profusely and told her that she'd gotten me off the hook since I knew I couldn't and wouldn't comply with her original desire. We talked about her fears, and I told her that I'd make sure we monitored her pain carefully and kept it under control. We also began the first of many conversations about what might happen after death. Comforted and reassured, my mother never mentioned suicide again.

Make Your Case and Keep Offering Support

The discussions are not always that smooth, of course, and you may feel tremendous pressure to go along with someone's dying wishes against your better judgment. Remember that you're under no obligation to agree to anything that is illegal or violates your own moral code, and if your loved one clamors for something in that category, acting from the heart means acting with integrity and explaining why you can't go along with the request. At the same time, it's imperative to keep talking and keep offering company and support in other ways, instead of shutting off communication.

All my experience with the dying tells me that fear and despair can become unbearably heavy when carried alone, and working to crack the shell of isolation that can silently surround a dying person, even in the midst of friends and family, is one of the most significant aims of acting from the heart. That shell can look like a wall built by an impossibly stubborn person who can't be reasoned with and seems only to want life to end. It can look like rage or take the form of requests that seem deeply distressing to you.

But to act from the heart is to remember that you are here to support and want the best for this difficult person, too. You can disagree, or be hurt or perplexed by your loved one's actions, and still offer kindness, honesty, and love.

For instance, you may be faced with a loved one given very little time to live who insists on pursuing a potentially painful intervention whose costs on every front, you believe, will far outweigh the benefits. In such a case, acting from the heart translates to making your case for why you think the treatment is a bad idea. That could sound like the following: "Mom, I think the surgery will reduce your quality of life because of the pain involved. At best, it'll give you another month or two. I understand it's what you want, but I'd encourage us to think things through together and see what really makes sense. You asked me what I'd do in the same situation, and the best I can tell you is that I'd allow nature to take its course. I'd want effective pain management and to be surrounded by those I love."

I'd suggest making your case lovingly at least twice, perhaps three times, explaining what you believe is the best option, which one you'd choose for yourself, and why. You can do this at intervals, saying things such as "I see that you're angry/upset. What I'd like to do is wait a couple of days, so you can think things over. Please know that I love you very much and want to help in any way I can. Talking things over will help us clarify the situation, so we can come up with the best solutions. You know how special you are to me. And, I want to make sure we give your concerns all the time they deserve."

However, once your loved one makes a decision—even if you think it's the wrong one—then I believe that the most loving and helpful thing you can do is to support the other person in having what he or she wants, in this case a successful surgery and as little pain as possible. The choice is not yours, and once the other person has made it, what's left to say is that he or she has your love and encouragement, and that you hope things work out as well as they can.

Ultimately, as long as the other person is competent to make a decision, he or she still has agency in these final days. And when he or she exercises it, it's important for family and friends to communicate "I'm still on your side, and here for you, whatever you decide." That's acting from the heart.

How to Act from the Heart in the Midst of Conflict
AN EXERCISE

If you're faced with the turmoil of holding strong opinions about your loved one's choices that create conflicts within you, and between you and the other person, bring yourself back to your heart, and the idea of service, before you take action. Start with this brief centering exercise and then ask yourself the questions that follow.

Center Yourself

1. Take five deep, slow breaths. With each exhalation, clear your mind of any concerns about acting from the heart.

2. Take five more deep, slow breaths. Each time you exhale, feel your heart open with feelings of love toward the dying person.

3. Take five last deep, slow breaths. With each exhalation, feel the joy that will come from acting from the heart.

Tap Your Heartfelt Wisdom

1. What does my kindest and wisest self say about what to do to serve my loved one?

2. What worries do I choose to let go, so I can act from the heart in service to the other person?

3. How will I feel as I act from the heart to serve my loved one? Allow yourself to fully imagine taking that action.

4. How would I feel if I refused the call of my heart and failed to act in service to my loved one?

5. What is the kindest, most loving action I can take now to serve this person?

Trust yourself and your wise heart. Your best will be good enough. Don't be afraid to offer it.

The Power of Heart-Centered Action

Acting from the heart in service to your loved one can profoundly change you. You get to see, close up, how agonizing life can be, how fickle, random, precious, and sacred it truly is. At times, you learn that both of your lives can become illumined and ennobled. As we act from the heart, we meet each other as reflections of a single, caring consciousness, a kind of loving wholeness that's big enough for our wounds as well as our peace and happiness.

It can take tremendous courage to offer your service to a friend or family member in this way, but I encourage you to act from the heart rather than hoping to fix or help your loved one. When we serve each other as equals, we shouldn't try to conceal or avoid our pain or confusion; the experience we share becomes an impetus to healing. And healing is always available to us, even when curing is impossible.

Chapter Four

I Will Treat You with Empathy

THE 4TH COMMITMENT

*I will use my imagination to put myself
in your place and try to understand what you
must be experiencing. I will let myself feel that
and keep that connection to you.*

What does your loved one need most right now? It's possible to listen, speak, and act from the heart and still miss an essential connection with the person in the bed. That's because it's so easy to unknowingly stay locked in your own thoughts and assumptions rather than feeling your way into what your loved one is experiencing.

You might walk into the room and project your own fears onto the other person, imagining, for example, that he or she is terrified or depressed, when that's not the case at all. You might say something such as "Things must be so hard for you," and, in return, the other person might give you a puzzled look and say, "No, not really. I'm doing all right. Today's a good day."

Or, you might become overly solicitous, assuming that if you were nearing death, you'd want someone to keep your room spotless, tell you how great you are, ensure that you always have your favorite things around you, and anticipate your every need. Actions such as these might annoy and sadden a loved one who misses the version of you who could tease, reminisce about old adventures, and act like the person he or she knows.

In this time of life, we see just how much we build our relationships on assumptions—assumptions about "what we always do"; the role we play with the other person; how the other person will look and behave; how we're supposed to act around someone with a terminal condition. But now, even the smallest assumptions can fail us because the landscape keeps shifting. Between one visit and the next, your loved one may be in a completely different physical and emotional place. There might be new information about how the disease is progressing or how the body is responding to treatment. A much-anticipated guest might fail to come by, or a cherished goal might suddenly seem unreachable. Pain subsides and then surges back. Crises come.

Hopes and disappointments, then pain and peace. Each visit is a new encounter, and you can't count on the familiar rhythms of your relationship anymore—or easily establish new ones—which is a little disorienting sometimes. I remember well how I'd talk to my brother when my mother was dying and be startled to hear him say, "She was doing fine when I saw her yesterday morning. She was in such good spirits." I'd think he was crazy because when I'd seen her not long after, she'd been sad and withdrawn.

That's why it's so important to be able to empathize— to put yourself in the other person's place each time you're together. As you're trying to stay connected with your loved one through the waves of changes that come, empathy will help you keep your balance more than almost anything else.

By empathy, I mean the ability to let your heart be touched by the feelings of the other person and allow his or her experience to resonate inside you. When you do that, your loved one's perspective becomes clearer to you, and you can find something in yourself that recognizes what he or she is feeling. So much happens when you feel that recognition. It creates a connection the other person can feel, a bond that communicates, "You're not alone. I'm with you in this." This connection doesn't fix anything; it doesn't offer solutions or look for silver linings. But, it makes both of you feel better.

You can strengthen your empathy by actively imagining yourself in the other person's place, opening yourself to what it might be like to have your loved one's condition unfolding in your own body, mind, and emotions. As you observe what's going on in the room and sit with your knowledge of this person who is so intimately familiar to you, you can bring yourself into the other person's world and try to look through your loved one's eyes.

You'll need courage to step close to death in this way. But if you are willing to feel your way into your loved one's journey, you can give your friend or family member the extraordinary comfort of feeling accompanied, understood, and deeply and compassionately loved.

Listening with Your Whole Self

Empathy flows from attentiveness, a kind of listening that involves our whole being. Mothers with small children attune themselves to murmurings and moods and stirrings in the dark, and that sort of tending often comes back at the end of life. We sit at a bedside, watching expressions flicker over someone's sleeping face, or notice a pause in the conversation and sense something important waiting to be said. We breathe in these moments, feel them in our own bodies. And sometimes, we discover meaning in actions that didn't make rational sense to us, or that might have escaped our notice if we weren't paying attention with our whole selves.

I remember being asked to help the nurses on the cancer ward deal with a difficult patient named Mario, a tough Italian-American longshoreman who was driving everyone crazy with the music he was playing in his room. Mario insisted on listening—at top volume—to the same handful of arias over and over. Both the nurses and his family thought that it was his way of somehow punishing them in order to push them away. No one understood what had come over him.

A Shanti volunteer named Bill Sullivan helped solve the noise problem by suggesting that we get Mario a headset, and with a hunch that bloomed into empathy, I helped solve the mystery of Mario's obsession. While standing in line to pay for the headphones, I began to wonder what it was that so captivated Mario about those particular arias. He seemed transported as he listened. He didn't just turn up the radio to annoy people; he had *chosen* these pieces—and it seemed important to figure out why.

I asked Mario for the titles: "E lucevan le stelle" from

Tosca, "Vesti la giubba" from *Pagliacci,* "O mio babbino caro" from *Gianni Schicchi,* and "Un bel dì vedremo" from *Madame Butterfly.* My mother loved opera, and when I read her the list, she told me that Mario's selections were some of the most beautiful and anguished arias she knew. Each one spoke of abandonment, grief, and the pain of dying. For example, in the aria from *Tosca,* a man awaiting execution sings, "Forever my dream of love has vanished. That moment has fled and I die in desperation. . . . And I never before loved life so much." The other pieces were similarly pointed, and poignant.

We finally understood what Mario had been trying to communicate loud and clear, what he hadn't been able to express any other way. Immersing himself in the music, he had been facing the end of his life with passion. With beauty.

Mario spent many hours listening to his music in the weeks before he died. And because we knew the pieces' significance, they led us into deep conversations with him about life, love, courage, and remembrance. The last time Bill visited, Mario wanted to hear *Madame Butterfly;* an hour later, he took his last breath, the music still sounding in his ears.

As you listen to your loved one with all your senses, with empathy, you may discover the meaning embedded in silences, casual comments, or behavior that seems inexplicable. When you intuit that something important is going on, follow your curiosity and ask the other person about what you're noticing. Sometimes you'll be off base, and your loved one will tell you. And sometimes you'll find that you've discovered a bridge between you, one that pierces the isolation and brings you closer.

The process of imagining what's going on with the other person, then asking if you're right—I think of it as course-correcting with questions—is at the heart of empathy. I've always found it to be my most important ally in easing the loneliness of dying people.

Learning Empathy

It's tough to be present emotionally day after day. I found that as I worked with patients and families in the cancer ward and sat at the bedsides of my own loved ones, I had to remind myself to keep trying to feel what the other person was feeling as closely as possible because I could easily check out and become detached or afraid.

Sometimes before visiting, I'd summon my empathy by imaging the loneliest and most anxious experiences of my life. I remembered times when I was very young, hearing my mom fighting with the neighbors across the alley in Brooklyn as I sat in my room alone, terrified. I didn't know whether I would survive if the adults around me kept screaming at each other. What if they hurt each other? What would happen to me? I could still feel the panic and loneliness in my body, so many years later. I took that understanding with me to the bedside, and when I saw those emotions in the eyes of a person who was dying, I recognized them, *knew* them, and wanted to bring comfort.

When my dad was in his final days, I would sometimes lie down in the bedroom near his room and pretend that I was the one who was dying of liver cancer. I could feel the animal terror in my body coming through me in waves, and my strongest desire was to have my loved ones around me—to keep me company, to monitor my pain, to talk and remember. I was grateful to be at home and not in the hospital. As I imagined all of this, I wanted more than ever to be with my father, no matter what.

There's a close link between our bodies and our emotions, and research on mirror neurons has shown that we have an ability to internalize the emotional state of other people by mirroring their body language. That's why physically lying in bed, pretending I was dying, gave me such a strong sense of what Dad was experiencing.

This kind of role-playing can be intense. So when the feelings of sadness and fear that came up became extreme, I kept myself from being overwhelmed by bringing myself back to my own life. "You're okay," I'd remind myself. "It's not your time. You can get up and walk around whenever you choose. You're doing this for Dad, to understand him better. Breathe slowly. Count to ten. Feel your love for Dad."

Anyone can do these sorts of experiments in empathy, and I found them to be so valuable that they became part of the training for Shanti volunteers. The following visualization exercise is one we used for many years to give people a deeper, more personal understanding of what the dying are experiencing. If you're moved to try it, you'll find that it gives you a sense of the whole spectrum of emotions that are part of the dying time and can bring you very close to your loved one.

Death Personalization
AN EXERCISE

This guided visualization is designed to let you imagine your own dying time as a way of feeling what your loved one is going through. You know the experience from the outside. This will let you feel it from the inside. You can create an audio recording of the visualization and complete the exercise as you play it back, but it's fine to simply read sentence by sentence, pausing after each one to feel and imagine. Afterward, you may want to write in a journal about what you've experienced or complete the exercise with another person and talk about it.

If you are feeling overwhelmed with emotion right now, save this for another time. Know that you are free to step away from the exercise if you need to. And remember, the things that come up as you do this visualization will help you connect with your loved one in a deeper way.

∘ ∘ ∘ ∘

Close your eyes and take some slow, deep breaths. Now imagine that you are in your dying time.

Imagine that you have been grappling with cancer for several years. Now, you are one month from the end of your time on Earth. You are in bed, at home or in a hospital, weary and alone. What are you thinking as you look around your room? What are you feeling?

Take as much time as you need to allow any images, thoughts, and emotions to fully emerge.

You've lost weight. How does your body feel? How do you look? What feelings come up when you see yourself in a mirror?

Spend time in this body and feel its reality.

∘ ∘ ∘ ∘

During these difficult times, who comes to visit you? Who is most helpful? How so? Among those you would have liked to count on, who doesn't visit?

Now, picture those you've loved most in the world. What feelings accompany the image of each one? What do you want from them now that your dying time has arrived?

Turn your thoughts to the work you've done for others, to contributions and sacrifices you've made on their behalf. How does recalling this make you feel?

Finally, as your time comes to an end, picture your epitaph. What words will be your final gift? What best captures the wisdom you'd like to leave to the world? Now return your awareness to the room.

∘ ∘ ∘ ∘

If you've tended to think of your loved one's needs primarily in terms of the demands of the disease or condition, this exercise should help give you a more complete sense of the anxieties and questions that clamor at this time of life. You can carry the empathetic understanding inside you to your loved one's bedside. In addition, your loved one might appreciate discussing the concerns that you imagine you'll have during your dying time. Listening and speaking from the heart when coupled with your empathy for your loved one will likely guide you to conversations that he or she will appreciate and find supportive.

What Might I Be Experiencing in This Situation?

You can keep opening yourself up to your loved one by remembering to ask, "What might I be experiencing in this situation?" That question was one I used every day in the cancer ward and frequently with my own loved ones at the end of their lives. It's a simple way to shift perspective, get to the heart of confusing or troubling situations, or put yourself in a position to notice what other people may be missing.

I spent time at the hospital with a fifteen-year-old girl named Sally who had advanced leukemia. She longed for her family, and though her mother came to see her often, Sally was hungry for comfort. I could feel her loneliness in the midst of the nurses and doctors who streamed in and out of her room, and her smile pulled me into her room anytime I walked by.

"I used to be a great softball player in high school," she told me as we sat talking one afternoon. "I could bat .900, but then my batting average started to fall. I was batting .500 and then .400 and finally I couldn't hit the ball out of the infield. I had to bunt."

I smiled at her and said, "Well, sometimes even the strongest hitters are better off bunting."

"So I guess I don't have to hit a home run every time. I just have to get on base, and it doesn't matter how." Sally continued, "You know, Dr. Garfield, the one thing I have to watch out for?"

"What's that, Sally?" I replied.

"I have to make sure I don't hit the ball to third base."

"Why?"

"Because if you hit the ball to third base you're dead. Third base is the coffin corner."

I turned away for a moment, struggling to hold back tears. I asked her what the coffin corner meant to her now, and she began to talk about how afraid she was of dying and how isolated she felt from her parents and the medical staff.

I called her folks to arrange what I called "What's on Sally's Mind?" sessions, so she wouldn't have to bear her worries alone. In one of those sessions, it came out that Sally had always felt like the apple of her father's eye, and that she believed she was disappointing him by being sick. That's how she read his infrequent visits, and simply putting her feelings into words allowed the two of them to give each other the support they both needed so much.

I know you're neither a psychologist nor an outsider to your loved one's situation, but by listening with empathy to what's being said and what's not—listening between the lines—you can feel your way into what it would be like to be in the other person's position.

Keep in mind that when you're caring for someone you love a lot, your capacity for offering comfort is greater than in situations where you don't care as much. You know this person. You can interpret a look, a grimace, a familiar phrase. You're uniquely qualified to find out what your loved one needs the most and act from the heart in providing what you can.

Each of us brings something different to the person in the bed—a different perspective, a different history—and your ability to empathize with your loved one may allow you to bring comfort in ways that other people can't. That's why your presence, even as a casual friend or acquaintance, is so important. On this particular day, you may be the one whose joke or touch or comment lets the person in the bed feel less alone, less afraid. You may be the one who hears someone like Sally say, "I need my dad," and be able to serve the whole family by letting someone know.

You won't, and can't, be the perfect, empathy-radiating companion all the time. No one can. We're human and we shift from love to fear and back. When your own fears of death come up, you'll start feeling glad that you're not the person in the bed and notice the way your fear divides you from your loved one. You'll catch yourself and return to looking, as best you can, through the other person's eyes. Don't walk on eggshells, afraid of making some mistake. Your loved one has more on his or her mind than your imperfect attempts to show empathy. You've both survived each other's screw-ups. The important thing is to keep reconnecting.

You Can Empathize Even if You Don't Agree

Your loved one may surprise or puzzle you with the way he or she looks at death—and that may pose a particular sort of challenge to your empathy. Many of us on the cancer ward didn't know what to make of a remarkable young woman named Greta, who had an unusually sunny disposition. Greta was Swedish and had met her new husband while visiting relatives in the United States. She married him, had a baby soon after, and then was diagnosed with advanced lymphoma. It was a terrible blow for a twenty-two-year-old mother with a nine-month-old son, yet she was unfailingly positive. Insisting that she was in God's hands, and He would take care of everything, she asked me if she could visit other patients "to help them with their troubles."

The nurses were suspicious. "We're not sure what's going on, emotionally," one of them told me. "She's always 'just fine.' Come on—there's got to be something."

But the more time I spent with Greta, the more I could see that her belief and trust were genuine. Still, it was hard for me to understand that at first. We were very different people, of different beliefs and dispositions, just as you and your loved one may be.

"I walk and talk with God each day, and I know that no matter what happens, I'll be okay," she'd say, with a kind of grace that was far removed from the fears I knew I'd likely have if I were in her shoes. Where did she get that kind of faith? I knew I wanted to learn about that from her, and as I became curious about her, my subtle judgments about how she must be naïve or pretending fell away.

Yet, I continued to share the nurses' concern that though she didn't talk about any anxieties, she must have harbored some about what she was leaving behind. I decided to mention that to Greta and asked her if we could talk with the medical staff, so they wouldn't worry about her. At the meeting, she reiterated her faith to us with a smile, but as she went on, clouds began to emerge. "The only thing I worry about is my baby," she said quietly. "Who will take care of little Tommy?" She regarded us for a long, silent moment. "Then there's my husband. Why is he afraid to come up here?" Her voice suddenly broke. "Why can't he find strength to spend time with me?" She began to cry, her sobs filling the room.

With Greta's permission, I called her husband, Rick, and arranged to meet him at a restaurant near the hospital. He'd been staying away, he told me, because he didn't know what to do or how to *be* with Greta in the hospital. Once I walked him through the door to her room, though, and he sat near her bed, Greta reached for his hand, eyes shining. Soon their heads were close, and they were whispering endearments like the newlyweds they were.

As empathy helps you see what needs to be done, and you check your perception with the person in the bed, you may find yourself extending your compassion, empathy, and support to another family member or friend whose presence your loved one sorely needs, perhaps inviting a visit. You can't dictate the outcome, but you may wind up giving your loved one a longed-for gift. Greta's condition improved dramatically after Rick began to visit her, and her cancer went into remission for a time, allowing her to go home to Rick and the baby. Those months, in which she could share her love for them and plan for Tommy's future, filled her with peace.

We brace ourselves for the worst as our loved ones are dying, but we need to be prepared as well for unexpected, inexplicable grace. When you encounter belief like Greta's, greet it with empathy, even if it differs profoundly from your own. The gifts of the dying time sometimes come in the form of understanding—for the first time—the sources of another person's character and courage.

Handling the Grief

Opening yourself up to the reality of your loved one's condition and concerns can leave you in a raw and vulnerable state. The same receptiveness that lets you enter the other person's new world from the inside also puts you face to face with your own fears of death and feelings of impending loss. You may find yourself grieving your friend or family member even as you work to comfort and serve him or her and maintain hope for the best possible outcome.

This kind of grief, called *anticipatory grief,* is a normal part of this stage of life, but it can leave you feeling alone. The other person is still alive, and you haven't given up on him or her. Yet, you may be coming to terms with the many types of loss you will face when your loved one is gone—not only the loss of the person but also the loss of the life and expectations, dreams, and, perhaps, stability that your loved one represents for you, or shared with you. You may feel sad, and also intensely angry, at times. To die is to lose everything that belonged to this life, and to be losing a loved one is to feel that loss as well as your own. Both of you may well be grieving as you let go of what has been and begin to accept what will be.

It sounds strange to say, but grief is one of the major things that connects you to your loved one right now. Nobody wants to make someone else sad, but sadness is built into these situations. Even when the person in the bed is at peace with death, there's always the sadness of leaving, saying a last goodbye.

I remember a family in which the beloved grandmother was calmly nearing the end of her long life. I came in one day to find one of her granddaughters crying. "I'm okay with her dying," the woman said, "but I'll miss her form. I won't be able to knock on her door and have her open it. I'll miss seeing and hearing and touching her. I won't smell her baking."

Tears are built into this time of life. Crying communicates that you care, and no one ever died of crying. It's okay to cry. If you're with the other person and feel tears coming, you can say, "I'm crying because I care about you and I'm sorry you're going through this."

Your emotions may come in waves, and you can swing from tearfulness to fear of what's to come, then to fury about what's happening. You may see your loved one suffering and wish for that suffering to end, only to feel guilty that you have somehow wished for death to hurry, fearing you have hastened it with that wish.

It's important not to hold in these emotions. If you have a friend or family member who can listen from the heart—without advice or judgment—it's cathartic and healing to talk openly about what you're going through and to express your pain. You can ask for support by saying something such as "I'm having a lot of strong feelings, and I don't need or want you to fix anything. I just need you to listen." A counselor, a hospital family group, or an online support group can be a particularly understanding outlet for the emotions you may feel uncomfortable expressing to someone who hasn't been through it. You may also want to keep a journal where you feel free to vent and can record the moments that have touched you, the memories that are surfacing, and the insights that you're gaining about the other person as you spend time together.

It's okay—in fact, it's vital—to step away from the bedside and leave the world of your loved one to return to your own. The pleasures of life that have always sustained you can replenish you now. Whether you blast music in the car, cook, read fantasy novels, or play with your kids, hold onto the thread of your regular life. Meditation and spiritual practice have proven invaluable to some people, running or movies to others.

It's not a betrayal of the other person to laugh, enjoy yourself, or feel joy. These, too, are part of the dying time, and when you can find them for yourself, you can share them with your loved one.

I know that holding your heart open to the other person with the kind of empathy I've been describing is difficult. Remember that the more you care for yourself, the more resources you have to care for the other person. This is not a usual time of life. The rules are different. It's natural to think, "If only this weren't happening, my good life would be here." However, this *is* your good life, and you are bringing great good to your loved one. Be gentle with yourself. Grieve if you need to. But don't let grief keep you from your loved one. Strange as it may seem, your pain creates an intimate connection between the two of you now—something I'll talk more about in Chapter 7.

Simple Empathy
AN EXERCISE

I'd like to leave you with one last exercise that can help you build empathy for your loved one's experience. It's shorter than the Death Personalization and meant to be used regularly, if you find it helpful. You can do this visualization at home before you visit, as you sit at the bedside during a silent moment, or as your loved one sleeps. I find that it can bring a comforting sense of peace and connection.

○ ○ ○ ○

Close your eyes and take three long, slow breaths,
emphasizing the exhale, then let your breathing return

to normal. Slowly turn your attention to the fact that this is a time when your loved one is suffering.

How do you feel as you focus on that suffering? Feel it as if it were your own.

Allow yourself to feel warmth and tenderness for your loved one, and as you focus on him or her, also allow yourself to feel any aching sensations in your body.

Now, taking long, slow breaths, visualize your loved one. Picture yourself extending a warm ray of light from your heart to the other person, a warm light that lessens his or her suffering. Feel this ray of light link the two of you and reduce the suffering you feel with each exhalation.

With this light connecting you, silently recite these words: May you be free from this suffering. May you be happy and joyful.

Repeat that wish as long as you like, no less than six times. Then feel your feet on the floor, take a deep breath, and open your eyes.

Allow yourself to continue to feel warmth and tenderness for your loved one. Let your wish to take away your loved one's suffering fill your heart.

Let that intention, that empathy, guide you.

Empathy Is a Gift in Itself

Henri Nouwen, the wise Catholic theologian, talks about the power and comfort that come when another person can tell us, "I am human, fragile and mortal, just like you. I am not scandalized by your tears, nor afraid of your pain. I too have wept. I too have felt pain." When you feel this empathy in your body, it flows through you as you hold the other person's hand or listen with all your senses to what he or she is communicating.

You may well be moved to translate your empathy into compassionate action—to take the step of saying, "Now that I understand, to some degree, what you're experiencing, I'll do my best to serve you." I know you will. But remember to keep connecting from the inside to the other person. Feel first, *empathize* first, then listen, speak, or act. Your heart will guide you.

Chapter Five

I Will Value
Small Acts of Kindness

The 5th Commitment

*I will value small, kind actions that
give you comfort and pleasure and not
tell myself that only dramatic, extravagant
gestures will have meaning for you.*

---

*T*he nurses on the cancer ward asked me to see if I could find out what was wrong with a man named Steven, who had developed a reputation for screaming at anyone who came into his room.

"What are you, some kind of social worker?" he snapped as I sat down in a chair near his bed.

"A psychologist," I told him.

"So now they think I'm crazy? Because I hate the way they buzz around me? You want to help? Go get some orange juice.

They said the chemo would make me thirsty, but I didn't know it could get this bad. I've been pushing this damn buzzer for half an hour!"

I'd thought I was there to use my training and experience to get at the root of some psychological problem, and maybe I was. But first, the guy needed juice. He was a changed man when he'd finished drinking the two glasses I brought him, calm and happy to talk.

I never forgot, after that day, that it may take only the tiniest of things—a swallow of juice, a touch, a joke, a song— to elevate the well-being and demeanor of the person in the bed.

We sometimes imagine that our most important job in being with dying loved ones is to marshal our energy and have a "big" conversation that will help them put their life in perspective, arrive with the perfect gift, or arrange just the right bucket-list surprise. But often I've found that small, everyday acts that bring relief, comfort, contact, and, perhaps, a little joy mean the most. You may think, "All I'm doing is sitting here or bringing along a few photos," but such gestures can be filled with meaning for your loved one.

I think small kindnesses act like trim tabs, tiny rudders attached to the large rudder of a ship. Moving the tabs, which takes no effort at all, creates vacuum pressure that turns the enormous rudder and steers the ship. In the same way, fetching ice, sitting together to watch a favorite TV show, or quietly reading at the side of the bed and being there when your loved one wakes up can create dramatic, positive shifts in mood or outlook, making someone feel loved and cared for, sometimes creating an enveloping sense of warmth and inner peace.

Adjusting Our Sense of Time

One reason small actions reverberate so powerfully on a psychological level, I've come to believe, has to do with how they affect our sense of time. During the last months and days of life, people are frequently alone, lying in bed or sitting in a chair, suspended in hours that have been emptied of to-do lists, goals, and "doing." The present feels like the painful place where the clock is steadily ticking down, so dying people escape from it in cycle upon cycle of thoughts about the journey of the past and the painfully limited future. And, so do those who wait with them.

But, the giving and receiving of one small act of kindness can pull both of you back to the expanded moment where what matters most is not what's being lost but what remains: your connection, your feelings for each other, the quality of your relationship. You can enter a space that's governed not by the ego that's watching time run out but by the soul, which senses eternity. In that space, you know what the soul knows: Life is fragile, and brief. And what counts is the love you feel and express as well as the meaning you give to what's happening right now.

I know that sounds lofty; it may seem like a huge leap from getting someone ice chips or reading to him or her from a favorite book to "entering the realm of the soul." But when you are fully with your loved one, offering small comforts, sharing stories, and bringing the gifts of self that only you can give, you are speaking the soul's timeless language of healing, and even transcendence.

We walk through everyday life trying to not know it could all be over in a heartbeat. But in the dying time of a loved one, we understand. We see. And with awe and respect, we feel the preciousness of every minute. It's that knowledge that gives so much meaning to any small action you take with the intention of serving and sharing love with the other person.

As that awareness rushes back, it may well bring both of you a sense of the boundlessness that comes with love. I've had many powerful, heartfelt connections—even with relative strangers—over the years, moments when each of us felt an unexpected sense of inner peace, even joy. We stopped dwelling on the losses of the future and let ourselves drop gently into each other's loving presence, which is always here, waiting for us.

Small Actions, Seismic Effects

I think we often know what sort of small, kind actions might have meaning for the other person, or offer him or her a respite, but we hold ourselves back from offering because we can't shake the question, "Will it be enough?" We worry that given the substantial challenges presented by the dying time, our loved one will find our offering petty, even insulting.

That's the tension between the ego and the soul: the ego saying, "It's got to be big and lifesaving to matter," and the soul saying, "Your gift of self is *all* that matters." When we allow ourselves to appreciate the beauty of giving from the heart, however small the act, we go beyond self-consciousness and truly reach out to our loved ones. What I frequently repeat to Shanti volunteers is "Don't talk yourself out of your best ideas, no matter how insignificant they seem. Make sure you don't disqualify your small acts by thinking, 'What good will it do?' Trust your impulse to give." Or, as Mother Teresa said, "We cannot do great things on this earth, only small things with great love."

I don't make a distinction between offering emotional support—listening from the heart to someone who is hurting, sad, depressed, or angry—and practical support, such as running errands or cleaning up. Practical support given in a generous spirit can be an intimate way of saying you value someone, and it lifts the other person emotionally. Emotional support can be extremely practical, renewing your loved one's spirit and allowing him or her to keep carrying on. These concrete expressions of love help give the other person a sense of a life well and fully lived despite the circumstances, a life in which he or she is appreciated and loved.

At the Cancer Research Institute, I'd often make a point of showing up regularly to watch a particular TV show with patients—a ballgame, or a soap opera, such as *One Life to Live*—and then we'd comment and recap. It got both our minds out of the pain and suffering and allowed the dying person to "remember what it was like to feel normal again," as one man told me. For the time we were together, the person in the bed laughed, relaxed, looked relatively okay, and had a short visit to the kingdom of the well.

Dealing with the twists and turns of a disease or condition that's advancing can feel new and strange, but kindness is a familiar part of being human and in a relationship with someone, and your small acts provide a sort of continuity in the midst of the disruption. They're a way of saying, "Despite everything, through all this, we're still us, being good to each other."

Doing Small, Helpful Actions
A FEW GUIDELINES

What thoughtful action will delight or uplift your loved one? That will change from day to day. But if you ask and listen from the heart, as well as listening *to* your own heart, you will know. To help you see other possibilities for serving your loved one, here are a few guidelines and suggestions for small kindnesses.

If you're visiting, it's best to call ahead and be sure the time you've chosen still works for the other person, whose energy and condition may fluctuate. If you're not a member of the family or a caregiver, plan to keep your visit brief—fifteen minutes to a half hour is a good length—to avoid taxing the other person's energy.

Most important, remember to make eye contact, sit down to take your loved one's hand, and listen from the heart anytime you visit. If that's the only thing you do, you will already have offered the profound kindness of making caring contact. In addition, you might

- offer to write down what visitors say, so your loved one can read their comments later or talk about them with you;
- take a short walk together, if your loved one is able;
- offer to read aloud a book or magazine or play some entertaining podcasts;
- drop by with photos of your garden, your child, the people at the office, or the new building going up down the street. You can bring the world and its stories into the room;
- watch TV, movies, comedy clips, or YouTube animal videos;
- offer an arm or hand massage, if your loved one is comfortable with your touch. You can bring lotion and warm your hands by rubbing them together or running them under hot water;
- bring a music player with your loved one's favorite music. I brought my mother a small CD player and her favorite classical pieces, which I played for her whenever I visited. The old technology served us

well, since she was able to look easily at the CD covers and could ask her hospice aides to put on a specific recording whenever she wanted to hear it;

- put together photo albums, which can be vehicles for memory and conversation. Your loved one may especially appreciate an album of photos that includes notes from you that detail specific sensory memories: "I remember polishing your black work shoes with your shoeshine kit and then shuffling around with the big boats on my feet"; "I remember our old house on Plum Street, and how I'd sit on the porch by the rosebush, waiting for you to come home"; "I remember how I'd pretend to be asleep in the backseat because I loved it when you carried me in from the car";

- decorate the sickroom with your loved one's favorite photos, artwork, or children's/grandchildren's art;

- read cards, emails, and phone messages to your loved one;

- create a personal website on Caring Bridge (caringbridge.org), where you can share updates on your loved one's condition and receive comments that you can show or read to the person in the bed;

- record messages for the person to listen to. A moderately priced service called lifeonrecord.com makes it possible for friends and family members to call an 800 number and leave their stories, reminiscences, and good wishes, which you can replay over the phone and save on a CD or online;

- bring along a favorite food your loved one can still enjoy. Good coffee or frozen treats that can be shared in the moment can create a sense of delight on occasion;

- review vacation photos. My mother and father loved to talk about trips they'd taken. Travel made them happy, and remembering places around the world they'd seen transported them out of hospice and into faraway journeys;

- ask if your loved one would like you to bring in some stationery for notes to friends and family, if he or she has always sent cards. You can take dictation, and he or she can have the pleasure of sharing a kindness with someone else;

- do the dishes or a load of laundry while your loved one sleeps;

- feed pets or help coordinate their care; or

- relieve the primary caregiver or bring food for visitors and the care team.

We don't always know how our gift will be received given the powerful circumstances in play for our loved one, but my experience has been that, in by far the majority of instances, small acts have been greatly appreciated.

You may feel that you have little to offer, but the act of giving is vital, especially during the dying time. So, I'd ask you to consider: What small act of kindness might you offer your loved one? Don't be afraid to remember, or laugh, or say, "I love you."

Gifts Only You Can Give

In the long months when my best friend Rico was dying of multiple myeloma, we had the chance to revisit some of our favorite memories and places. Mostly, we'd take walks, when he was up to it. We'd walk and sit, walk and remember, walk and talk about women, or politics, or sports, or dying. We talked about our lives, mostly.

At one point, when he had rebounded a bit, I suggested that we do one last, easy workout to celebrate and honor our three decades of friendship and being workout partners at the gym. He loved the idea. We did all our old exercises and reminisced about the times we'd had at the gym. He talked about "our last workout" several times during his final weeks, once remarking, with obvious joy and fulfillment, that "we were strong, young men."

For my mother, I put together three small albums filled with family photos from before I was born, and even from before she was born, until the current day. We'd page through them together, and she looked at them frequently when I wasn't there. The images triggered numerous conversations about our lives and the people in them, and the hours we shared recalling specific events and comparing our memories were some of our most treasured times together.

You may not have a deep or layered history with the person in the bed, but it doesn't matter. If you were the friend who used to go to your loved one's house for cooking lessons or meals, you might now ask your friend to divulge some recipes or techniques you can record and pass on, or watch chef competitions on TV. If you have been professional colleagues, you might want to talk shop. There are gifts only you can give: stories, shared passions, your particular sense of humor or outrage or fun. Reminders of these things—who you are and what each of you brought and still brings to the relationship—are precious. Share *those.*

Your compassionate presence means everything. I can't say it often enough: the most important act of kindness is for you to simply be there with an open heart.

Small Acts of Kindness Are Healing for You, Too

Thinking in terms of small kindnesses can seem absurd or ridiculous in the face of your loved one's situation, yet it can give you a way forward, a set of next steps.

I was contacted by the parents of a six-year-old boy who had been diagnosed with a rare form of leukemia and given six months to live. The mother was distraught. "This is so unfair," she told me. "We're churchgoing people. We give to charities and collect food for the food bank. What else should I have done? Is there a God? Should I pray for a miracle? Please tell me something to ease this pain and outrage."

"If you focus on the hurt you feel and the inexplicable way this pain has come to someone you love so much," I told her, "you'll retreat into yourself and miss the opportunity to spend time together, time that will seem precious later on.

"The best thing you can do for yourself is to focus on making every day special for your son. Offer favorite tastes and snacks, and favorite activities when that's possible. Look into his eyes often, and enjoy his company."

The mother told me later that something had shifted inside her as she turned her attention to trying to add "something special" to her boy's days. It wasn't that she could bring a pony or offer trips to Disneyland, and she knew she didn't have to. She could simply be Mom for her dying child, comforting him through the difficult times, sharing small delights. They savored simple treats and wrapped themselves in the comfort of each other's company until the end. You, too, can do this, remembering that the most treasured gifts are the ones that communicate, "I see you. I know you. I'm here."

Giving in this way takes away some of the feeling of helplessness that can set in as we watch our loved ones weaken. We want them to stay as they were, and sometimes it can feel easier to turn away than to see them as they are now, frail or suffering or diminished. But, small kindnesses can spark happiness in them, and in us, and we see that we can keep connecting, spark-to-spark, no matter what's happening in the body.

You don't have to be a member of the family or part of someone's inner circle to make this connection. At Shanti and the Cancer Research Institute, a sense of us—you and me—developed during my time with patients. We were comparative strangers, yet the sense of intimacy that flowed between us seemed quite similar to what I later felt with my mother, father, and best friend during their dying times. I'm not saying the depth of loving was precisely the same, but rather the connection I felt with people on the cancer ward was far stronger than I expected, and it was created and expressed largely through small acts of kindness.

These small actions sustained me. When I saw the effects of a kind comment, a touch, or a small gift, I felt less like a failure who should have been able to prevent the mistake of the other person's dying. I felt like a good person who was doing everything he was able to do. I could somehow accept that dying comes to all of us—and that we are *alive* until our final breath.

Each time we offer a small act of kindness, we remember our loved ones are dying. Still, we can feel tender toward them, even laugh with them. They are dying and we have time together—right now—that we can approach with love.

Do Your Best to Put Expectations Aside

There may be unspoken hopes and expectations attached to our gifts. All of us want them to be well received, and to hear words of appreciation. We may think that we can heal a strained relationship with our loving words or small gifts and visits, or that we'll finally win praise we've been hungry for all our lives. However, that's far from a given.

Your loved one may be consumed with pain, stress, fear, or loneliness, unable to enjoy, or perhaps even to notice, your kind gesture. I remember spending a good deal of time on one of the photo albums I made for my mother and felt pleased because I knew she hadn't seen some of the photos in years. I left the book with her, thinking about how delighted she'd be. But, no remark was made on the gift. It sat untouched for a week, and I couldn't help feeling disappointed, and a little taken for granted.

I had to remind myself that Mom had been struggling with disease-related symptoms and probably didn't have the energy for anything but getting through another day. The generous adult part of you will know this when your kindness seems to go unacknowledged, or is greeted with a half-hearted "That's nice, dear," but you may also have to contend with a part of yourself that wants the gift to be noticed and appreciated right away. It is useful to remember that dying people have a great deal of empty time when they sometimes replay the day's happenings and remember the kind things that were done for them. A delayed acknowledgment sometimes comes after that sort of reflection. It wasn't uncommon for my mother to thank me a day or two later for something I did for her.

Mom eventually did pick up the neglected photo album and was looking at it one day when I came in. "It's delightful," she said. "Let me tell you about some of the people in those old pictures."

But it can happen that thanks are sparse, even nonexistent. That may reflect your loved one's personality or lifelong patterns in your relationship. Old dynamics in families or among friends don't automatically go away during the dying time. My mother saw me as the one who "excelled" at caregiving, which translated as *expecting* many small acts of kindness from me in addition to what I did as her primary caregiver and partner through her illness and time in hospice. She didn't have the same expectations of my brother or ask as much of him—even though he's a loving, compassionate, and highly competent man.

Inequities like this don't feel fair, but they persist. If they come up now, try to look at them with compassion and see if you can find forgiveness, not only for longstanding patterns but also for any unfairness that arises during these final days.

If your small acts of kindness seem to fall into a black hole, it can be heartening to direct some toward people who are likely to notice, need, and appreciate the glow of your giving—

caregivers, medical and hospice staff, and others who are sharing this time with you. Their happiness will feed you and make it easier to keep showing the love that can bring your loved one peace.

Send Waves of Kindness and Appreciation Through the System

Just as a small stone dropped in a pond lifts lily pads far across the water, one small kindness can ripple through the whole community that's come together to support the dying person. Others in the room feel cheered, and even visitors who come to the bedside later seem to sense it.

One reason this happens is that receiving and witnessing acts of kindness physically changes us by triggering the release of oxytocin, called by some the "love hormone." Oxytocin can increase one's sense of self-worth and optimism, as well as lowering blood pressure. When you set it flowing in your loved one's room, it can create a "pay it forward" attitude, as your friend or family member smiles at a nurse, who jokes with a visitor, who says something loving to a family member—each one spreading the warmth.

I'll always remember the time I brought my mom, already in her dying time, several boxes of Skinny Cow ice cream bars.

"I love you very much," I said. "Here's a supply of your favorite treats."

She smiled broadly. "I love everyone!" she said. "I want *everyone* to have a Skinny Cow, especially the new patients here at skilled nursing, who may be scared."

Each time a nurse walked by, a visitor stopped in, or someone stuck his head in the room, Mom sent me to her freezer to get an ice cream bar. Her face lit up as we handed people their treats and sent them out with more to take to others. For that time, she and I weren't worrying about her condition or thinking about death. We were filling up the skilled nursing floor of St. Paul's Towers in Oakland, California, with love.

Mom talked often about that day before she died, and I still smile to think of it. We reveled in other people's surprise and pleasure, and it left both of us feeling joyful.

There can still be lightness at the end of life and a desire to give. Simple activities such as that Skinny Cow afternoon can produce "peak experiences," to use psychologist Abraham Maslow's term, that fill us with awe, wonder, and a pervasive sense of peace that makes us grateful to be alive. Jonathan Haidt, another psychologist, thinks of peak experiences as "a manifestation of humanity's 'higher' or 'better' nature," and he describes how they trigger a "helper's high" that is both physical and emotional, with a warm feeling in the chest, a sensation of expansion in the heart, an increased desire to help, and a greater feeling of connection with others.

Small kindnesses renew you as well as those around you. Extra thank yous, small presents, and "I love yous" can become the norm. Generosity can blossom, even now. Especially now.

Aristotle observed that happiness and fulfillment are the result of "loving rather than in being loved." My mother's experience with the Skinny Cow ice cream bars showed me how beautifully love can be expressed with something as small as a bowl of jelly beans or a box of one-dollar ice cream bars when you follow the impulse to give them away.

Chapter Six
I Will Listen to Your Stories

At the end of life, most of us want to live on, somewhere, somehow. I think that's why it so often happens that a kind of autobiographical momentum builds, a desire to remember the life we've led and, if the opening arises, to share our stories so they'll be retold and woven into the fabric of memory and history.

That's not the only reason life stories surface now, of course. People want to make sense of what they've done and find understanding that may have eluded them. Our stories define us, label us, burden us, and liberate us. A woman at eighty years old may still see in herself "the girl who cheated on the test" or "the one who loved her children better than her husband." A dying man's memory may riffle through scenes of "the defiant son" or "the father who was never home" or "the guy who never had the guts to go for it." There may be no looming angel standing at the threshold between life and death asking us to explain ourselves. But in that liminal, twilight space, many people pause to review the stories of how they've used their given days, examining moments from the distant and more recent past, evaluating their choices, and calling *themselves* to account.

The lonely hours of the dying time fill with memory and judgment, regret and pride. That life review is one of our final tasks, and it often happens in solitude, unspoken. I've found, though, that immense comfort and closeness can come when people are encouraged to tell their stories, and we see those stories as a legacy that we can learn from and preserve.

The memories that emerge now have the power to transform both the speaker and the listener. We know that, and yet storytelling can get crowded out by the pain and uncertainty your loved one and you may be facing. Some people assume that because the person in the bed has always held his or her stories close, nothing will come of asking for them now. Or, they're concerned about how to respond to what they hear, and what to do with the thoughts and feelings triggered by the other person's observations. But if you're willing to listen, share your own stories, and speak kindly from the heart about what you hear, feel, sense, and remember, you'll open the way for both of you to talk about what has meant the most to you—and perhaps find the wisdom there.

Coaxing Stories into the Room

Conversations about the past often start spontaneously, with your loved one offering a memory of "the time the car broke down in the desert" or "the way you used to put kittens in the mailbox when you were little." Or, they may flow from something happening in the room right now, with both of you watching a football game and the other person looking up to say, "Remember how I taught you to throw a pass over the hedge in the backyard? I was so proud of you."

The past is nearer than ever during the dying time because the future, which occupies our minds so much during the rest of life, is truncated, and the present may seem to offer more pain and challenges than comfort. So memories rise, along with the question, "Who was I, really?" Threads of reminiscence may naturally start to cohere into a review of your loved one's life. But if they don't, you might simply ask the dying person to tell you his or her life story. You can record, and even transcribe, the results and create a small book or video for your loved one and those close to you.

But it's the stories themselves and the *listening*—not any document—that are the treasures. People during their dying time have often said, "Remember me," knowing that our memories of them will keep them from ceasing to be and allow them to speak to the future.

When I asked my dying father to share his most important memories, he jumped at the chance. "There are people and events I don't want to die with me," he told me. "I'm the only one who remembers them now and I want to pass these memories along to you."

We spent three long sessions of nearly two hours each— with breaks for him to rest—recording his early years, his marriage to my mother, the birth of my brother and me, our early life together, and his later years.

I was lucky—he spoke easily, using the storytelling skills he'd developed as a salesman. But if he'd been reluctant, I might have coaxed him forward with questions. You can't force your way into anyone's memory, but you can invite recollections by saying, "I'd love to hear about your life, and, especially, the times in the past you remember most," or "What stories do you recall from your life that are most important to you now?"

Then you can ask questions, such as the following:

- What did the house you grew up in look like?
- What was your experience of school like?
- Which people were most important to you when you were little?
- How did you meet your husband/wife?
- What motivated you to start your career?
- How have you changed since you were a teenager?

Later, you might segue to additional questions:

- What memories make you most proud? Most thankful?
- What kind of person do you think you are?
- When people think about you, what would you like them to remember most?
- If you had your life to live over, what would you change?

Responses to questions such as these can lead to a life review that takes in the sum of your loved one's days and acts as an honorable means of closure, as well as a way of saying goodbye.

My father seemed to feel complete after we had walked through his life together. When we were done, he took my hand in his, raised it to his lips, and gave the back of it a long kiss. "Now, you won't forget me," he said. "Just listen to the tapes, and you'll remember everything about your old dad."

Why Storytelling Is So Important

Dying people often tell stories about their lives to find meaning in what they've experienced, and they feel grateful when those stories offer insights to family and friends as well. It is not unusual for them to discover through storytelling that issues they've wrestled with in love, relationships, careers, spirituality, or parenting, for example, have been alive for decades. Patterns and connections—some of them new—emerge in stories seen from the end of life. A man who has always thought of himself as unlucky might begin to notice moments of unexpected grace or generosity that give him a new perspective. A quiet woman who has always envied her more outgoing siblings might realize that her temperament created a valued refuge for herself and others. Someone else might recognize that fear, not circumstance, is what held him back.

When you listen without judgment to what comes up, you make it safe for the other person to look at perplexing life concerns and work through challenging emotions. Deep truths, traits, and themes that have played out unconsciously over a lifetime can become visible and emerge as a connective thread that gives a sense of coherence, and even purpose, to choices and events that had seemed random or inexplicable. Ideally, both of you will start to sense the vital core of the narratives and tune into their deeper messages.

Your loved one stands at the center of these memories, learning from them, being changed by sharing them. That process is what's crucial, not how any particular story ends.

Some of the most important memories aren't inspiring or easy to share. Nevertheless, they reflect the dying person's truth and the essence of a life. That's why, as my friend Rachel Remen has observed, "Everyone's story matters. The wisdom in the story of the most educated and powerful is often not greater than the wisdom in the story of a child, and the life of a child can teach us as much as the life of a sage."

Their Truths Can Touch Your Core

Stories can create intimate bonds as we catch unexpected glimpses of ourselves in the mirror held by the other person.

One of my most profound teachers on that point was a man I didn't know was dying, a stranger who shared his story with me. I'd gone to Paris at a confused moment of my life, feeling lost, and visited the Cathedral of Notre Dame, hoping for inspiration. I sat on a back pew, waiting for a long while, but the clarity I needed eluded me, and I got up to leave, discouraged.

As I walked through the heavy doors onto the cathedral steps, I passed a man in tattered clothes; he smiled and extended his hand as I greeted him. "Did you find what you wanted inside?" I asked him.

He studied me for a moment. Then he said in heavily accented English that he'd first traveled to Paris many years ago, fleeing from a tragedy in his life. "I wanted God or Mary to tell me why I should continue to live," he said. For weeks, he'd prayed daily at Notre Dame but received no reply. "I was lonelier than ever and wanted to die."

His money almost gone, he decided to stand outside the cathedral and ask people for help. That first day, a kindly nun brought him food and said she would pray for him.

"She was my first friend, and she returned many times."

The next day, a boy gave the man a few coins, and later brought him food. A few weeks passed, and one evening, as he'd sat nearly alone inside the cathedral, the South Rose

Window began to glow and a wave of joy took possession of him. "I heard a voice that seemed to come from inside and outside of me at once," he said. "It was the voice of God. *Continue to pray and meet new friends,* He instructed. *Soon, I will come to you.*" He held my eyes, smiling. "Would you like to know what happened?"

I nodded.

"Nothing!" He laughed at my expression. "Nothing at all, except that each day someone has spoken to me as a friend, just as you did."

I laughed too. "How long have you been out here?"

"Nearly thirty years," he said. "I will stay as long as I live. Each morning before the people arrive, and each night after they leave, the Fathers allow me into the cathedral to pray for the good fortune of all my friends." His warm voice lingered on the final word.

I asked if he still felt lonely.

"No, I have no reason to be," he said. "I talk with God each day. And when I gaze into the eyes of a friend, I know that it's God looking back at me. Yes, my friend," he said, "we are all faces of God, especially when we speak with open hearts to people who are troubled and alone. Then, it is God speaking to God."

Every judgment I might have had about him at first glance—that he was to be pitied, that he was probably depressed, that this life couldn't possibly be of his own choosing—dissolved. The intimacy that came with hearing his story brought me closer to him than to people I had known much longer, but with whom I hadn't entered such depths. And, I continue to be inspired by the wisdom he offered me. The soul-to-soul connection he was describing as the center of his life reminded me that it was my life's work as well. It is, after all, what comes when we listen, speak, and act from the heart.

He showed me something else that might comfort you, as it did me: Pain doesn't have to break you. It can open you to something much larger. What looks damaged on the surface can be quite different on the inside, and the wholeness—the spirit—inside is always there for us to see, if we take the time to look.

I was shaken when I returned to the cathedral on my next visit and learned that the man on the steps had died. I'd known him for perhaps half an hour, but I felt that I had lost a cherished friend.

You may think that you have heard every one of your loved one's stories, or, conversely, that his or her true nature will remain forever hidden to you. However, your assumptions may be as flawed as the ones I had of the man on the steps. When we make ourselves available to the wisdom of our loved one's stories by listening and speaking with an open heart, we encourage the other person to tell them, unencumbered by the fear of judgment. There, we may find dimensions of a loved one that we've never seen or expected. And, we often discover new dimensions of ourselves.

Healing Can Blossom as You Listen

The fact of mortality sits heavily in the room when you're with your loved one. I was very aware, as I sat with my dying parents and best friend, that it would be me in the bed at some point, and that it *wasn't* me right now was only a matter of chance and timing. Quietly, I took stock of my life, just as my loved ones were doing.

My mother talked often about her difficult relationship with her own mother, who was quick with criticism and didn't express her love easily or often. It was a wound she'd carried with her all her life, and as she spoke, I thought of how difficult our own relationship had been. Dealing with Mom had always been a challenge for me. I didn't bring that up as I listened; however, I acknowledged it to myself and realized that she and I had something in common that was deep and important. I felt closer to her then, and as she felt that, she drew closer to me. Healing often happens in this way—with witnessing, with a shift in feeling, without words.

As you listen from the heart to the stories you hear now, you are allowing the possibility that even in these final days, your sense of the other person—and yourself—can be enriched by new information, new interpretations, new connections, and, sometimes, a new kind of understanding or acceptance. Abraham Maslow, the psychologist, talked about the way the human psyche isn't all darkness, even in the darkest situations, and how there are always opportunities for us to be more than we think we are. I've often seen the truth of that as people share stories in the dying time.

Jacob, a man I met through Shanti, was seventy-five years old and nearing retirement when he was diagnosed with advanced congestive heart failure. He had spent his entire adult life working eighty-hour weeks to give his family a life of ease, dreaming of the years he'd have to relax with his wife and sons and enjoy their company. Now, he was depressed and full of regret for how little time he had spent with them over the decades he had been "married" to his work. His sons, for their part, were angry and resentful about having to care for a father who had been largely absent for most of their lives.

A perceptive social worker encouraged Jacob to talk with his sons about why he had focused so single-mindedly on work for so long, and, for the first time, the sons learned the details of his early life. Jacob's family had been torn apart during the Holocaust, and he had spent more than two years in Nazi death camps. "I escaped by the skin of my teeth," he told them. He had promised himself then that if he married, he would keep his wife and children as far away from want and suffering as he could.

Part of the decision to insulate his family from any trace of what he had experienced led him to immerse himself in his business, so he could lavish them with material comforts. The same impulse kept him from "burdening them" with stories of the horrors he'd endured during the war, though the experience had defined him. It's not uncommon for loved ones to find that they've been "protected" in a similar way from difficult, pivotal episodes of a dying person's life— whether they're experiences of war or loss or trauma.

When Jacob finally told his story, he and his sons, David and Albert, cried together. He told them how much he loved them and apologized for not having been a greater presence in their early lives. Then, he asked for their forgiveness. Jacob's final months became a time for love, healing, heartfelt conversation, and mutual understanding. It was clear to his sons that their father's strength and devotion to his family were traits that he'd passed on to them.

I keep Jacob in mind when I urge people to create an environment, through listening and speaking from the heart, that encourages the one who's dying to reveal his or her most important truths. Had Jacob kept his stories hidden, his sons would have known only the man who "abandoned them for this work" and never understood what he'd given them.

The Puzzle, and Possibility, of Self-Forgiveness

As people review their lives and begin to bring up pressing memories or transformative insights, I've noticed that one unavoidable theme is forgiveness. Remembered failures and transgressions can feel overpowering now, and remorse, even fear, can loom large. But as you listen and speak from the heart, it's often possible to help the dying person find perspective that makes forgiveness, particularly self-forgiveness, possible.

I once took care of a Roman Catholic sister named Marie who asked me what I thought about heaven and hell and wanted with the urgency of a true believer to go to heaven.

But on several occasions, she told me that she had not been a perfect person, or a perfect nun, and was haunted by times in her early life when she had done things she was not proud of. Crying, she told me she was not a virgin; therefore, she ought to go to hell. She had never told anyone that, she said, and now she was remorseful and afraid.

"I'm not a believer in the kind of afterlife you've described," I said, "but one way to go from hell to heaven while you're still on Earth might be to forgive yourself."

Something opened up between us after that, and we were able to talk with much greater ease. She knew I was not a Catholic, and that I was much different from her, but it didn't matter. I trusted my intuition about what to say, and it turned out to be important for her. She didn't need an outside force or authority figure to forgive her—she realized she could forgive herself.

If you get a sense of what it would be helpful to say if your loved one talks about regrets and wrestles with the lessons to be taken from them, trust yourself. If it feels both true and kind, speak from the heart and share it.

It can be particularly difficult to hear loved ones say they wasted their lives or failed to realize their dreams, but I've found that most people who express such disappointments are speaking about particular sadnesses, not the entirety of their lives. It's important to allow them to express their feelings about these regrets—then encourage them to remember times during which they felt happy and fulfilled. In my experience, even at their saddest, people are willing, even excited, to talk about the people, things, and times that made them feel happy and content.

It's also helpful to point out that many, if not most, of us have regrets, which is a part of life. You can say things, such as the following, when a loved one talks about regret:

- "It's not fair to judge your actions or inactions of the past using insights and awareness that you have as a more mature person. You were who you were then, and now you know more and see things more clearly."
- "You did the best you could have done with the information and resources you had at the time. If you look at your entire life, you'd likely agree that not all of it has been wasted, that there also are some things— no matter how small—that still make you proud."

As people re-examine the fullness of their lives, more often than you'd think, "failure" turns out to be a label that doesn't really fit. I remember sitting with my father, both of us recalling how hard he'd worked and how much of himself he'd given the family. He'd been told more times than I can count that he'd fallen short and never reached his potential, but, in fact, he'd been a good provider, both financially and emotionally. Neither of us had seen the story of his life that way, but it seemed so obvious now that I was moved to say, "Dad, you were great at the job that counted the most— taking care of us." His eyes filled with tears as he realized it was true. With that simple reframing, a lifelong shame and perceived weakness was transformed into a source of pride and gratitude.

Old narratives often lose their hold as we sit with each other, thinking about our lives together and sharing stories. It can be disconcerting, and painful, to hear people at the end of life say they failed at something important to them, or wish they could go back in time and redo, or undo, an action that bothers them now. But I found, as I sat listening to the dying, that it often helped to remind those saddened by what they'd done or left unfinished that *I* was learning from their experiences, and that I would do my best to share that wisdom with others. I've heard so many people's regrets at the end of life—"I wish I had spent more time with loved ones. I wish I had pursued my passions. I wish I had trusted myself more. I wish I had ventured out, risked more, put myself first more often, given more, loved more." And each time, I've felt myself looking carefully at my one singular and precious life, feeling the urgency of living it.

The dying bring home to us that all we have is now, and, as John Updike put it, "There is no then." To honor that clarity in your life is to honor them in the most meaningful way—by carrying that wisdom into the world.

Your Stories Can Remind You Both of Who You Are

The power of stories to connect us makes them a potent antidote to the stresses that build during the dying time. I remember talking to a woman who had been caring for her husband in hospice and felt increasingly distant from him.

"Should I feel guilty because I'd like some expression of appreciation from him?" she asked me. "It's been such hard work, especially at my age. Of course, I wouldn't have it any other way, but he's so angry. He's angry with God for giving him cancer, and I think because of that he snaps at me. . . . We've always been a loving couple with so few bumps in the road. What can I do?"

Frequently, anger is the only emotional response strong enough to ward off the anxiety, the terror, of what's happening.

But even though her husband seemed consumed by it, their relationship didn't have to be.

"You've had a loving life together, with great stories to tell," I told her. "Sharing them will help remind you both of the warmth you've forgotten."

The suggestions I gave her will help you, too, if you find yourself and your loved one mired in negative emotions.

- Don't be afraid to address the negative feelings directly by saying something such as "If I were in your situation, I'd probably be scared at times, and one of the ways I deal with fear is to get angry. I love you even though you're angry with me."

- Ask the other person if he or she remembers a time when you were both really happy. Pick an occasion you know means a lot to the other person—the day your children or grandchildren were born, a trip you took, your wedding—one of the times in your past that brought you closest. Photos from those moments can prompt recollections for both of you.

- Begin to tell your stories of that meaningful time. Your loved one, similar to the woman's angry husband, may become intrigued by your memories or be pulled into a desire to expand on those stories and, once again, be one of the people who enjoyed those happy times.

- Invite the other person's memories. You can go deeper by asking, "How does that time look to you now? Does it seem as though it's from a former life? After all, it really was your life."

Perspective can change in important ways when we become a witness to the story instead of the actor in it, and that's true whether you're reviewing old times or telling the story of life right now, the rough stuff that you're both living through. It's amazing how quickly and effectively some people can create a meaningful and coherent story from their current situation and shape painful circumstances into something purposeful and nourishing.

The angry partner of the woman I was counseling came away from listening to her stories of their first meeting, their family, and their travels saying, "We really did have a happy life," and expressing gratitude for their time together, past and present.

You May Not Always Like What You Hear

I don't want to romanticize the kinds of insights and interactions that come up as stories are exchanged at the end of life. Sometimes, it's not easy to hear what the other person has to say or suspend the judgments that come up.

A few months before she died, my mother told me, "I hated you when I first saw you after you were born." I was shocked by the comment—my stomach clenched under the emotional punch, and my mind raced. How could she think of saying such a thing to her son, who, by the way, was caring for her so diligently?

When I could finally get words out, I said, "Why would you hate an innocent little infant who had just gone through a difficult birth and was just reunited with his mother?"

"Because getting you born was extremely painful," she said, with logic that seemed oblivious to my feelings. "You weighed over nine pounds, and I was a small woman. The pain was unimaginable."

"Well," I responded after a long pause, "I'll forgive you for hating me if you'll forgive me for causing you pain. I'd really like to wipe the slate clean after all these years."

A lot happened in the moments before I spoke. As I took deep breaths to steady myself, I thought about what I wanted to accomplish. Here was my mother, whom I loved, who had just unconsciously assaulted me with a comment on her deathbed. It shook me, but I reminded myself that I was the healthy one, not burdened by all the stresses of being in the dying time. It served no purpose for me to get angry, withdraw, or hold a grudge. We'd had some beautiful moments filled with loving exchanges, and this comment was an exception. It hurt like hell that she'd hated me, but instead of getting caught up in a mental argument, I focused on breathing deeply and slowly, and as my body calmed down, I realized I could let the hurt go.

If you find yourself reeling after an unthinking wallop from the other person, I recommend grounding yourself as I did and taking a break if you need to. Try not to get angry and harm the relationship. Think of how you'll feel after your loved one dies if you spin into negativity, so do your best to respond with empathy and loving kindness. I know that may not be easy.

I once cared for a man named Andre who was dying of metastasized prostate cancer. He told me that as a young man decades earlier, he often had sex with younger, less mature women. Casting himself as a louche hero, he boasted about how he built them up with flattery and attention, then lured them into going to dances with him and parking alone afterward in remote locations. He'd manipulated these women and treated them as prey, but he insisted that the sex was consensual and bragged that he'd attracted them with his good looks, clever ways, and sexual prowess. When I asked him if he regretted hurting so many innocent people, he shrugged his frail shoulders. "Everyone had a good time," he boasted. "No harm, no foul. Besides, all's fair in love and war."

It was hard for me to stomach. When I commented, "I'm glad I never had a sister who got hurt that way," he smiled and replied, "It was such a long time ago."

A principle that has guided me, and the many volunteers I have trained, is that no one deserves to die alone, and that has allowed me to keep speaking and listening from the heart to people like Andre, with whom I would never spend time otherwise. But, if you're faced with a family member who has hurt you or those close to you, and who continues to be abusive or share stories that trigger the worst in both of you, remember that *you* don't have to be the one to keep the person company at the end. You have the opportunity to seek some kind of resolution, but if it doesn't come, you also have the opportunity to leave.

Say Andre had dated my sister and hurt her badly. I might have reminded him of that fact and said, "I'm carrying a lot of anger toward you because of what you did to my sister. I'd like to talk with you about it, so I could find some forgiveness in my heart. Is that okay with you?" If he agreed, I would ask, "Do you ever wonder why you did those things to my sister and the others? What thoughts or feelings do you have now as you remember those events, times, and places? How does it make you feel to share this memory with me?"

It's quite possible that a person faced with direct questions like that might express regret and want forgiveness for actions taken years or decades earlier. Perhaps Andre, approached that way, would apologize. If he didn't, I would still try to find a way to forgive him and tell him something such as "I want you to know that I don't condone what you did, but I forgive you as best I can and I want to keep visiting you. What do you think?" If he wanted to continue our visits, I'd do so. If not, I'd wish him well and try to connect him with someone else who didn't have the burden I had.

If I couldn't find any forgiveness for him, I would tell him, "I'm sorry, but I still feel awful about what you did to my sister years ago. It would be best for both of us if someone else came to visit you."

Because of my background and personal values, I would likely let him know that if he really wanted me to stay, I would swallow hard and not abandon him. But if he had a number of attentive friends or family members to care for him, I'd give myself permission to see him less often.

We all have to live with our choices, and it's important to be true to yourself as you act from the heart. The bottom line for me is that when I can, I want to do my best to minimize suffering. Even people who have acted poorly deserve compassion, and it makes me feel better to give it. You have the right to decide what's right for you.

A Chance to Rewrite the Ending

Why put yourself through the discomfort of talking about old hurts or disappointments? I encourage families to do it because although the past can't be changed, the present gives them a chance to draw closer.

One of the most meaningful exchanges I had with my mother before she died began when I was moved to tell her, "I hope you forgive me for anything I might have done that upset you—now or in the past." That started a conversation about our relationship in which we forgave each other for things— some large, some small—that happened both recently and long ago. I was surprised by what she was holding onto and similarly surprised by some of the old hurts I brought up— going back to elementary school—that I forgave her for.

In the end, we both expressed gratitude for having gone through this life together as mother and son. The last time I saw her, and it was obvious she was dying, we were able to say goodbye to each other with kindness and love.

Any negative history you have with the other person matters, and I'm not suggesting that you discount it. However, the past is not your potential. Important growth and change can result from the poignancy of the dying time, and I've often seen that people don't necessarily die the way they've lived; they can develop into better people than they ever were.

If your history with another person is especially troubled, a counselor can help you think about what it would take to create a sense of peace and closure. It doesn't happen magically or automatically, but it's worth exploring.

Stories Allow Us to Endure

For many years, I've seen the relief and joy on the faces of people at the end of life as they've spoken to someone who listened from the heart about their experiences, the people they've loved, and the parts of their lives that troubled or excited them. I've witnessed secrets, sadness, joy, revelations, and regrets, but what came up the most often were the challenges and satisfactions of love and work, memories of the everyday activities and relationships that carry so much of the meaning of our lives. These are the stories—many of them free of high drama and emotional fireworks—that so often convey the remarkable texture of a person's life.

Years ago, at the Cancer Research Institute, I cared for a retired high school teacher who loved to tell me about the students he was proudest of, kids who made something of their lives and attributed some or much of their success to the lessons they learned in his English literature class. He had saved their letters, in which they described their successes, and they let him know that he had been there at "just the right time" to guide them.

Their stories were part of *his* story, and he talked proudly about how much he'd loved these kids and tried to bring literature to life for them. He'd made it a point to recommend short stories, plays, and novels that had messages that would illuminate the issues in their lives, and he kept in touch with them after graduation, meeting with them to discuss their transitions and challenges.

To the end, he was the amiable professor—it was the identity that defined him and made him most proud. I remember our bedside "seminars," in which he'd slide into his expansive knowledge of human nature and literature and hold court. When I mentioned that I was struggling in my first marriage, he recommended that I read *Tristan and Isolde* and sent me to look again at *Romeo and Juliet.* That, he said, was the best way to think about love.

Our exchanges were warm but never very emotional. Yet, they glimmer in my memory when I think of him and bring him vividly to life. For dying people, that's one of the greatest hopes—that they'll endure inside us. The promise we can make is that we'll put our hearts into listening to the stories of who they were and remember them.

Chapter Seven
I Will Use My Pain to Connect with You

THE 7TH COMMITMENT

I will use my own wounds and pain to understand and connect with you. I'll talk honestly about what I'm experiencing, so we can comfort each other, reduce each other's suffering, and help each other heal our isolation and loneliness. I will care for myself as I do this, so I can better care for you.

Staying focused on your loved one, as you've been doing when you listen, speak, and act from the heart, creates an atmosphere in which the other person can feel less alone, less afraid. But *you* may feel isolated in your pain, as though you can't risk showing the fear and sadness and confusion inside you—or perhaps even let yourself feel these emotions—because you believe your role is to calm and serve, not complicate the situation with your own feelings.

Opening up about your experience, though, can allow you to connect with your friend or family member in a way that brings both of you out of your isolation. If you've been hiding your distress for fear of making the other person feel worse, it's important to know that you don't have to carry your worries alone or hold in your tears. You've shared much in life, and now, when both of you are hurting, you can help each other through this pain.

Quiet the Fears

It can be scary to acknowledge how your loved one's condition is affecting you, because doing so removes any protective illusion that you can insulate yourself from what's going on, and it requires you to confront emotions that you'd rather push away. Perhaps the most immediate of those is fear, especially the primal variety that can overtake you when you look into your dying loved one's face and see your own.

"My mom is in hospice with maybe a few months to live," a Shanti volunteer named Pat told me. "She's dying of breast cancer, which runs on my mom's side of the family, and I have to admit that breast cancer freaks me out. Am I watching myself die in twenty or thirty years? I have a hard time staying in the room or even visiting Mom. What can I do?"

You may be all too familiar with the escalating panic Pat felt as her mind launched itself into calculations about her own genetic odds and reeled with anxious thoughts about her "fate." "All of us deal with that when we stand so close to death," I told her. "As a young psychologist working with Stage 4 patients on the cancer ward, I was sometimes overcome with concerns about my own health and mortality and fought hard to restore my equilibrium. I found using a visualization exercise was one of the most effective techniques for calming my fear." I then provided Pat with a set of instructions, which follows, to help her be present with her mother.

Create a Mental Movie
AN EXERCISE

Start by doing the same breathing exercise you use when you stop at the threshold before entering the room—take ten slow, even breaths, counting each inhalation and watching your stomach rise and fall as the air moves in and out of your body. You can repeat this cycle of ten breaths two or three times.

Now, imagine yourself walking into the room and creating an easy, gracious connection with your loved one. Visualize yourself sitting calmly at the bedside, focused on listening, speaking, and acting from the heart. See yourself exactly as you'd most like to be when you're there—pulling your chair close and taking the other person's hand, maintaining eye contact, using all your senses to feel what's needed. Imagine enjoying the other person's company, free of anxieties.

You needn't spend more than a few minutes with this exercise, and you can do it anywhere, even as you pause in a hallway or before you get out of your car.

This kind of mental rehearsal is most effective if you practice regularly—preferably right before you visit—though you can do it at other times during the day as well. The brain and central nervous system can't tell the difference between a frequently practiced mental rehearsal and the actual physical experience. So the more you watch your mental movie, the easier it will become to quiet your fears and be present with your loved one.

o o o o

Pat told me later that she'd begun using the visualization exercise before entering her mom's room, and, occasionally, when she "felt the fear coming on," she'd excuse herself and meditate in the restroom before returning. She became calm enough to sit with her mother for lengthy visits, watching TV, reminiscing, and, sometimes, simply sharing the silence. "The fear is still here," she said, "but it doesn't always get the upper hand anymore."

Making Room for Openness

When fear isn't in control, it can become a part of the conversation with your loved one, and both of you can feel the relief of talking about what you're going through. Your emotional turmoil can't likely match that of a person who's dying, yet it gives you a visceral sense of what he or she is experiencing, an understanding that comes from the inside. You can share this the way you've shared so much else—if you are willing to put aside the persistent idea that acknowledging the pain will only make it worse.

I watched one elderly couple, married for fifty years, do an almost farcical dance of avoidance when I was working at the Cancer Research Institute. I knew from the wife's medical chart that her days were dwindling, yet her husband never said the word "terminal." In fact, he never gave any sign that he realized her condition was dire, or that he was terrified and grieving. He insisted that he wanted his beloved partner's remaining time to be happy.

The wife worked to protect him by glossing over her pain and hiding what she knew and sensed of her prognosis. Each of them maintained a smiling facade, and each was miserable inside.

The husband resisted when I took him aside and suggested that they open up to each other. "If I tell her the truth, she'll be crushed," he told me. "It will kill her even sooner!"

Reluctantly, he agreed to speak about what the doctors had told him, that her time was limited. I watched as he broke the hard news and let his feelings spill out.

"I've known all along," she said with a soft smile.

He stared at her. "You did?"

"Yes, sweetheart." She reached and pulled him close. "God, I feel so relieved to say it!"

Now, they could say farewell and spend her final days closer than they'd ever been.

The Difference Between Pain and Suffering

There's no way to bypass the emotional pain of the dying time. Dying people stand on the edge of losing all they have been, and all they've loved. They're angry, they grieve, and they fear the silence that will come when their hearts cease to beat. All of us do. And, all of us will face that moment. Yet even now, when the reality of death is so close, there's a tendency to resist it and say, "This can't be happening! Why me? Why us? How can this be possible?"

Dwelling on such questions can turn the shifting, changing experience of pain into a more solidified experience of suffering. Pain and suffering are often used interchangeably, but here's the significant difference between them: Pain is the raw experience—the anger, loneliness, exhaustion, and sadness that come and go as the body declines and we feel life waning. Suffering, though, is the prolonged, intensified distress that comes with struggling against the reality of the pain, seeing it as a punishment or believing that it's yours to endure alone. Pema Chödrön, the Buddhist teacher, puts it simply when she says that the nature of our lives is change—including the way living becomes dying. "But when we resist change, it's called suffering."

It's easy to spiral into suffering, especially if you hold in your fears and painful feelings and allow them to build. Many people are surprised at how relieved they feel when they accept that the pain exists and they let the dying person know, "Yes, we've been knocked down by fear and sadness and grief. Yes, what's happening hurts like hell. So how can we get through this together? What can we do right now to find solace, comfort, and closeness in the time we have left?" Because that's the choice: we can sit with each other in the heart of the pain and reach toward love and relief—bearing the dying time as a *we* instead of an *I*—or we can run from it and deepen the suffering.

What It Means to Be "In It Together"

A recent Dutch study of terminal cancer patients found that those who considered their suffering to be unbearable felt the most depleted by four factors: physical pain, weakness, loss of autonomy, and loss of meaning. Fortunately, I have seen, again and again, that friends and family can significantly reduce the intensity of each of these with a caring presence and a willingness to face and share the pain.

When there's physical pain, it's vital to call on the expertise of professionals, especially the hospice team. A core part of the hospice mission is keeping pain in check—and not only the pain related to the terminal condition. My mother's decades-long back pain decreased markedly when she was in hospice and finally got the kind of meds she needed to alleviate it. It was an unexpected bright spot in her later days.

We tend to think of relieving physical pain in terms of using the correct drugs in correct combinations and amounts, but here, too, attitude and support make a significant difference. Clinical research on pain in the dying has found that relief is intimately tied to the way people regard the pain. According to spiritual teacher Stephen Levine, if people see pain as part of the human condition and not an individual assault—thinking of it as *the* pain rather than *my* pain—they experience pain as less intense and easier to bear. Shared pain is easier to carry, and when you open up about your own pain, you help the dying person experience pain as something common to *all of us*. Drugs are powerful, but so are storytelling and empathy and touch.

Weakness—even more than physical pain—was the condition that made the Dutch cancer patients' dying time feel the most difficult to bear. That's troubling because it can seem as though there's little to be done when a loved one grows progressively weaker. Life is ebbing. Weakness is inevitable.

But, a direct mind-body connection colors the way the dying experience their weakness. When their bodies feel physically depleted by illness, they feel less able to advocate and care for themselves and they lose confidence in their ability to think well—all of which makes them feel even weaker. That's why it's so important for you to offer emotional support with words such as "We're in this together" and "I'll help you think through what's going on and make decisions." When a loved one feels strongly connected to you, and knows you'll be there to share the many challenges of the dying time, the sense of being "too weak to deal with all this" diminishes. The weakness that felt all-consuming begins to feel more manageable, less overpowering, because it's balanced by your strength.

You can build trust and connection by involving the dying person in conversations about what's going on, what to expect, and what he or she can still control. Seeing you as a partner in the decision-making makes it easier for your loved one to lean into you for support. Therefore, the suffering that comes with fighting the weakness and battling the loss of personal agency can give way to accepting or asking for more personal communication and help from you and others, the team that will help carry him or her through to the end.

When my mother and father were growing progressively weaker, I took on a kind of parental role for them, as many adult children wind up doing. I felt strong and they did not, so it made sense for me to step up and serve as a loving adviser. I didn't infantilize them but rather helped them hold the situation together, lovingly and clearly.

I talked with my father, for example, about the benefits of hospice, which he originally regarded as "giving up," even though his oncologist had estimated his survival time at three months. He didn't want extreme treatments or expect miracles, but he didn't want to hurry death either, and he associated hospice with "final days." I told him that I might choose hospice care if I were in his position, and I filled in details he hadn't known, such as the fact that if he lived longer than the six-month prognosis that qualifies people for hospice care, he had the option of leaving it, with his doctor's approval.

As he talked through the possibility with me, he began to see it as a smart and beneficial choice, a way he could make his dying time easier for all of us. The decision was his, and making it reinforced his sense that he was in charge of his own life.

You can offer this kind of support as your loved one confronts each new decision by taking the following steps. I've outlined them before, but I'd like to repeat them here.

- Make it clear you are "in it together"—you are committed to one another and to doing what is best for the dying person.

- Encourage your loved one to offer opinions about the choices at hand, and as he or she speaks, listen from the heart to what's said and left unsaid.
- Share the burden of decision-making by contributing your thoughts about "what I would do if it were me," but remember that this is the other person's dying time, not yours.
- When it's possible to do so, give the dying person the final say.

For my parents, being able to stay involved in their own dying time and direct what happened as much as they could increased their sense of independence and lessened their feelings of weakness. Sharing their stories and reflecting on their lives helped them hold onto a sense of meaning. They didn't succumb to despair or hopelessness, or fall into an abyss of loneliness. We stumbled, endured sadness that was sometimes overpowering, and dealt with physical loss after physical loss. But because we did it together, and shared the pain we all felt, we could help each other suffer far less.

Wounded Healers

When I talk about sharing your own pain with a friend or loved one, I'm not suggesting that you sit at the bedside, rend your clothing, and wail. I'm talking more about showing the other person that while you can't know exactly what he or she is experiencing, you understand it and are moved by it, because you have endured loss and fear and vulnerability in your life, too.

Even the smallest acknowledgment of what's broken you, and what you're going through now, helps the other person feel less alone and better understood. And as halves of an injured "we," it's often easier for both of you to be forthcoming about what's going on.

When I was losing my father, I felt my foundation, and my heart, shattering. As Dad talked about how much he had to live for and how he didn't want to leave everyone, I struggled, at first, against my despair and found myself saying things such as "It's okay. We'll do everything we can to be sure you have lots more time with us," or "You don't have to worry about us. Just think about getting better."

But as time went on, and both of us accepted the reality that he was dying, I finally let myself respond to his sorrowful statements by saying, "We're sort of in the same boat because

I'm losing my dad." As I did that, Dad no longer felt he had to protect me by pretending to be happy and telling jokes, and we could speak to each other with a new kind of truthfulness. For the first time, he began to tell me how he was actually feeling when I asked, and he felt freer to talk about what was on his mind. Often, he asked for reassurances that I'd take care of my mother when he was gone, and we agreed that we'd both do our best until, as he put it, he "reached the far shore."

You may not be used to talking this way, this openly, but taking the risk of sharing your sadness with the other person changes the terms of the conversation, and it may change the nature of the relationship as well. I was very close to my graduate-school friend Rico, a longtime workout buddy and fellow psychologist. Over the years, we often traveled together and talked sports and cases. But, we weren't the kind of guys who put our feelings about each other into words.

After he was diagnosed with terminal cancer in his early fifties, though, I felt compelled to tell him how sad it made me that his cancer was so unrelenting. "I'm here for the duration," I said as we sat together one afternoon. "It hurts like hell to be losing you, and I'm here for you any way you need me." I know he heard the truth and sadness in my voice because he looked at me kindly and smiled. Then, he took my hands in his and gave them a strong squeeze. Our relationship shifted then from one that felt close and collegial to something more intimate—a bond of brothers, best friends.

I told him often that I wished he didn't have to endure so much pain, and he said he appreciated words like that because they acknowledged what he was going through. He hated it, he said, when people told him he should be grateful to have had such a good marriage, such a good career. "It's their way of looking on the bright side—and distancing themselves from what's happening right now," he told me. It made him feel less isolated when people who cared about him didn't pretend away what he was experiencing, or bury their own feelings.

I often teach Shanti volunteers that they can connect with their gravely ill clients by seeing the other person's sadness, loneliness, and fear and talking about times when they've felt that way too. Such stories can soothe your loved one by saying, "I'm with you. And in some small way, I understand."

When my mother was dying, she spoke sometimes about how lonely she felt when her many visitors had gone. It was tempting to say, "Don't worry, I'm here," and at times that's what I did. But, she took the greatest comfort when I told her, "I learned from my divorce how hard it is to be alone and how grateful I was when someone close to me—or even a kind person I knew—showed up for a visit." It was a way of saying I couldn't take Mom's loneliness lightly, because I knew firsthand how much a visit from me, or anyone, meant.

A Different Kind of Healing

A certain feeling of helplessness can come as you share your loved one's experience. As you continue to let go of the idea of "cure" or "getting better," sometimes all that remains is heartfelt presence—and that may not seem like enough. But, never forget that to the person in the bed, it's everything.

I often think of Bharat Lindemood, the Shanti volunteer I've previously mentioned, who had a remarkable ability to comfort patients during the height of the AIDS crisis in San Francisco. He moved from bed to bed in a crowded AIDS ward, making contact, opening himself to what was going on in each room, inside each person.

Bharat vividly remembered a man who "stared, terrified, at a spot on the wall in the grip of a panic reaction about dying. The guy had AIDS-related pneumonia and couldn't breathe well. He was gasping for breath and really freaking out," Bharat told me. "He was trying to hang on, breathing laboriously and loudly, while fixating on a spot on the wall. His eyes were wide, and he was panicked. It was a graphic scene."

Other people might have fiddled with the man's oxygen mask, helped him to sit up, and stayed focused on trying to get him comfortable. "They might only see 'an agitated patient,'" Bharat said. "I saw terror, a fear of dying and that he couldn't catch his breath. And, it was all getting worse. The respirator was fast and loud, and there was an obvious struggle going on."

Bharat responded quietly, from the heart. "At first, I sat next to him and matched my breath with his, synchronized long and loud breaths," he said. "His mask made the sound of his breathing even louder. I was breathing *with* him. We were connected. I then stood up, leaned over him, and put my hand on his chest, breathing with him, matching in-breaths and out-breaths. I wasn't doing anything *to* him but, in a more relaxed way, I matched my breathing to his. I said, 'I'm here with you.' I didn't try to fix his breathing, but I just wanted to connect with him.

"I realized that it could have been me in the bed. I identified with his terror, his utter loneliness. There were no other visitors. It hurt to imagine myself in his situation, to know that it wasn't some experience that was foreign to me. I did for him what I'd want someone to do for me. Touching him was my way of getting beyond the words, truly connecting with him and his predicament—and hopefully his soul—emotionally and spiritually. By touching him and then expressing what I saw, I acknowledged and normalized his fear. In a way, I gave him permission to let go.

"I told him, 'What you're going through is what many other guys have gone through. They made it, and so will you. People I've known on respirators who were nearing their death but managed to stick around awhile said they weren't so afraid anymore.' I spoke my truth to him. I spoke from the heart about what I had seen and learned, and it calmed him down. His breathing got more regular, and he stopped staring at that spot on the wall in panic. I believe I reassured him. He died a few minutes after I left his room. He was on the precipice, on the threshold. Had I not been there, he might have died terror-stricken. I helped him approach the threshold with a bit more peace of mind."

You may find yourself overwhelmed by your loved one's condition, by the pain or exhaustion or tears. But at such times, true and loving words such as "It's hard for me to see you afraid like this," and "I don't know what to say or do for you, but I'm here; you're not alone," can help bring healing. They can't erase the condition or stop the dying, but in acknowledging your confusion, your vulnerability, they can help heal the agony of separation—both your loved one's and your own. At the bedsides of the dying, I've often said, "I've never died before, but I've been very afraid, and I think I understand a little of what you're going through." Those, too, are healing words.

Living with the Pain

Staying emotionally connected with your friend or family member during this time will require a lot of you. After all, it can mean accompanying your loved one on a descent into hell—going into the place where the other person talks about what hurts a lot, how unfair life is, how scared he or she is.

The pain you feel, as you share theirs, may be hard to manage. At times, you may try to wall it off, deny it or not feel it, and stay busy with the pragmatic duties of care, or retreat into parts of life where it's easier to have a sense that you're in control. But, it's hard to do that for long because any sense of relief that comes from trying to numb or distract yourself is quickly offset by your need to care for the other person—which I believe is as strong as your loved one's need for care.

A second approach is to open yourself completely to the pain you're immersed in. It may feel like the most compassionate thing to do, but the danger is that you'll become a reverberating chamber in which your loved one's situation becomes all-consuming, and you can't let go of what he or she has said and the pain you both feel. As that begins to happen, you may feel faced with the choice of suffering intensely and constantly or taking a break from visiting so you can regain your footing.

However, there's a middle way that can help you stay with your loved one without becoming overwhelmed: to be as fully present as you can when you're in the room and learn to let go when you leave. Doing this when you're away from the bedside is much like letting go of thoughts in a meditation. Yes, your mind will keep circling back to the conversations you've had in the room, the sadness, the questions you have about whether you're doing enough, and what life might be like going forward. But as in meditation, you can acknowledge these thoughts and concerns and release them—and you can get better and better at doing that with practice. One thought needn't become a cascade of thoughts. You can notice it and let it go, returning to the world in front of you, the soapy dish in your hand.

It helps to give yourself regular opportunities to completely change the channel by stepping away from the caregiving role and anything that reminds you of death. In the years when I was constantly at the side of the dying, I made a point of doing that. It was impossible to stay centered without taking breaks. I went to the gym, sat in the Berkeley Rose Garden, and took in the view of San Francisco from the top of the East Bay Hills. Sometimes, I watched clouds or the water. I made periodic lunch dates with friends and escaped into movies that didn't trigger strong emotions. I urge you to do this, too, by seeking out whatever feeds your own being—music, time with children or animals, being outside, cooking. Remind yourself of what you enjoy and make a little time to do it.

Beyond these brief breaks, I encourage you to get periodic relief if you are one of the primary caregivers. Arrange to take a break of a few hours, or even a few days, to keep yourself from becoming overwhelmed. Lean on the team of caregivers and potential caregivers around you—friends, hospice, and volunteers.

Separately, I strongly recommend sharing your pain with someone else—a caring friend, a therapist or counselor, a member or members of a support group. Doing that will lighten the burden you carry when you return to your dying loved one. You may come away with fresh insights, information, and pragmatic tips, but more than that, you'll see once more how much your experience is a part of the fabric of life, and how many of us share this pain.

Kristin Neff, a psychologist who's a leading authority on self-compassion, offers a useful observation: "Things will not always go the way we want them to," she writes in the definition of self-compassion on her website. "You will encounter frustrations, losses will occur, you will make mistakes, bump up against your limitations, fall short of your ideals. This is the human condition, a reality shared by all of us. The more you open your heart to this reality instead of constantly fighting against it, the more you will be able to feel compassion for yourself and all your fellow humans in the experience of life."

That's especially true in the dying time.

You'll probably bounce among ways of being with the pain—opening yourself to it and becoming overwhelmed, retreating, and going through times when you can let go. But, you can aim to spend more time in that balanced place where life goes on both inside *and* outside the room. It's okay, and necessary, to do that.

The key is to bring a depth of presence to your loved one and to find ways to enter an emotional space in which you are focused on listening, speaking, and acting from the heart from the time you cross the threshold until you leave. When you do that, you've done all you can. You've given all you can give, and it's okay to live the rest of your life, too. The choice is not between serving your dying loved one and serving yourself. It's between being able to sustain your compassionate care and presence and not. The more support you get, the more self-aware and resilient you can be, and the more you replenish, learn, and grow, the greater your capacity will be to serve your loved one. The opposite is also true: the more compromised your physical, psychosocial, and spiritual resources are, the more eroded your emotional resilience and mental stability will be, leaving you with less to give.

Day by day, remember: *Extraordinary levels of pain require extraordinary self-care.* It's vital to take extremely good care of yourself.

Each time you return to your loved one, you'll both be different. There's no formula for this time in your relationship. Be gentle with yourself. There are no perfect words, no right answers that will make things magically better. The more you simply allow yourself to be with your loved one, bearing the pain with him or her instead of pulling away, the more comfort you will offer.

You don't have to hold it together. You can break. That's how the light gets in.

Chapter Eight
I Will Allow Love to Sustain and Heal Us Both

THE 8TH COMMITMENT

I will help both of us look through the eyes of love at our pasts and anything that remains unhealed. I will keep you company as we share the mysteries of death and what comes next, knowing that love will always connect us.

The end of life is a time of letting go of the body and releasing the hope that we can somehow deny death. It can seem as though everything is steadily contracting, and the universe has shrunk to the dimensions of the sickroom, soon to completely disappear.

But even as the body's strength fades, along with a person's ability to do the things that have filled and defined a whole life, a new kind of growth is possible. When familiar roles, routines, and abilities are stripped away, we can come to know that there is more to us than our physical body, our accomplishments, and our history. In the quiet of the dying time, it's easier to hear the soul's message that the core of our being is love.

Love, the soul tells us, is what matters most now, and it's all that has ever really mattered. It connects us with each other, and with the Eternal, and it endures after we die.

Love can enable the dying—and us—to heal ancient hurts. Expressed in ways large and small, it allows us finally to reach a place of peace.

Friends and family can do much to encourage the soul's loving perspective to emerge, and they can help the dying person feel the presence of this expansive, timeless part of the self. Small acts of kindness can do this, as we've seen. So can using expressions of acceptance and love, especially the words "I love you." Touch, music, nurturing conversations about what happens after we die—these, too, can put us in touch with the soul's language of connection, transcendence, and eternity.

I know that treatments may continue and practical decisions need to be made. But above all, the soul tells us this is the time for love. A great blessing of this final stage of life is that the capacity for both expressing and receiving love expands. I've seen repeatedly that love is bigger than weariness, bigger than despair, bigger even than the terror of death. More than anything else, if you allow it in, love will feed and sustain both of you. And, when you are willing to enter the realm of the soul with your loved one, you will learn the great truth of the dying time: love heals.

Feeling Close Again with "I Love Yous"

You might see a bit of yourself in the note I received recently from a woman whose father was in the dying time:

> I'm exhausted. My dad has been living with my husband and me for two years. Recently he was given a terminal diagnosis, and now the hospice team is helping. But it still leaves me with a lot to do. I love my dad. We can't afford to put him in a skilled nursing home. Nor does he want to go. I'm getting on in years too. I'm afraid I may fall apart before he does. What do you suggest?

On the physical level, it seemed that the well had run dry. If only there were more money, perhaps there could be more help for her, better care for her father. If she had more energy and were younger, or if the decline had not been so long, perhaps then she would feel better able to continue meeting her beloved father's needs. But what was left now, in the last months of his life, was her fear that she had nothing more to give.

You may find yourself facing your own list of "if onlys." You may wish you had been closer to the person in the bed or you had come sooner or you had not given so much of yourself because you now find yourself worn out. But no matter how spent or inadequate you feel, words and acts of love can help you move from fear or regret to connection.

I explained to the woman that using the words "I love you" when she began to feel overburdened could remind her of her deep feelings for her father and soften the atmosphere as she cared for him. That may sound like very little, but as she began to say, "Dad, thank you for all you've done for me. I love you," she found herself taking more time simply to be with him, restored by the affection that began to flow again between them.

Now, instead of retreating into the roles of "the one who can't possibly carry this load" and "the one who's nothing but a burden," they could see themselves as daughter and father, two people who were there for each other. More than anything external, what both of them needed most was to feel genuinely connected to each other, and small expressions of love reminded them how to do that.

Love Keeps You Human

I know how much you may have been called upon to do for your loved one, and how much you still may be doing. I have always been struck by the way families and friends adapt to the needs of the moment and demonstrate their love by finding ways to meet those needs. They invent routines they've never had and adapt to the unexpected, growing into roles they've never before had to play—they tend wounds, change diapers, gently act almost as parents.

I saw caregivers during the height of the AIDS crisis handle cruel and distressing symptoms with matter-of-fact grace, making sure life went on: "So now this is happening. Okay, we'll deal with it." Through crises and panic and despair, they worked not to lose sight of the *people* inside the disease. I've repeatedly seen that there's so much more to the mundane, everyday act of caring for someone than meeting physical needs. Your endearments, touch, and coping routines reweave the ties between you, and they can carry you through to the end.

When "I Love You" Doesn't Seem to Fit

The healing power of love is available to you even when you don't feel particularly close to the person who's dying. Perhaps, you're caring for someone with whom you've had a difficult relationship or a person who has been lost in addiction.

If that's the case, I want to thank you for being the difference between zero and one for this person. Your presence is an act of love, even if you don't or can't label it that. So is every attempt you've made to listen, speak, and act from the heart. If you're struggling with the idea of trying to say "I love you" on top of that, you're certainly not the only one. Maybe you won't get there—you'll still be a good person. But, I hope you'll try.

A man I know, Brian, was in a similar situation. He'd grown up with a mother who'd told him since he was small that he was a "disappointment," "an underachiever," and someone who always "settled for less." His brother was a lawyer, but Brian went into the arts and supported himself as a waiter so he'd have the flexibility to go to theater auditions. He'd kept his contact with his mother at a minimum for years, but now, because his brother was "too busy," Brian was looking after her in her final days.

He wasn't used to being affectionate toward his mom, and the idea of telling her "I love you" seemed insincere at best. In his eyes, the reality was that they were "stuck with each other." He would do what he needed to do, he told me, but he didn't have to love someone who'd harped at him and made him feel inferior his whole life.

"If you don't think you can love her," I told him, "how about trying to love the spark of life inside her that gave you life? I know it hasn't been easy for you to be her son, but without her, you wouldn't be here at all. She helped you survive when you were helpless and she really does want you to be 'someone special.' That's what she's told you all these years. Maybe you can't love the way she's talked to you and how you feel when she criticizes, but see if you can love the life she gave you."

I asked him to try an experiment. "Just say, 'I love you, Mom,' without any concern for whether she reciprocates."

"You can't be serious," he replied.

It took several conversations before he was able to "let go of my mom's assaults" and see if he could "forgive and thank the dying woman who gave me life." He sat at her bedside, and, somehow, he got the words out.

"Mom, I want you to know I love you."

At first, Brian's mom, Anita, didn't respond, but then she looked at him and reached to squeeze his hand. He tried more "I love yous" over the next days and made a point of looking into her eyes when he did. His mother began to respond to his words by saying, "Me, too." As time grew short, something shifted, and Anita was able to offer "I love yous" of her own. Near the end, she told him, "I don't know what I would have done if I didn't have you taking care of me this way."

The healing that came through those exchanges was vast. "I finally knew that I wasn't a disappointment to my mom," Brian told me later. "We did the best we could during her life, and it was definitely difficult, but the end was a blessing for both of us. Now, I can carry our relationship in my heart as something really positive. Like you said, we were making memories at the end."

Responses such as Anita's don't always come, but even when they don't, your *attempts* to love the other person close the distance between you.

I suggested to Brian that Anita might now be a "citizen of Eternity," and that perhaps they'd meet again in some other time and place. "I'd like that a lot," he said with a smile, "as long as she's easier to deal with than the first time."

Shanti Moments

Love can lead both of you to a place where fear recedes into the background and nothing seems to be missing. During those times, there is no "me and you" but simply an "us" that fills your mind and heart. People often remember connections such as that as a kind of vital healing that leads them to a new place in the relationship. In these "Shanti moments," as I call them, we exist together in an abiding state of profound love.

I was permanently changed by such a connection when I was a psychology intern in a veterans' hospital. One of my first patients there was a man named Jim who had a disease called Guillain-Barré syndrome, which causes a spreading paralysis that can result in death. Jim seemed tiny in his bed, dwarfed by the equipment that helped keep him alive, and it was easy to see how intimidating it would be for those who knew him to see him that way. His family had mostly stopped coming to visit. Yet, he was fully alive and hungry for contact and conversation, so we talked about the life he'd had as a musician on the road and the fears that came to him as he lay awake at night, wondering how long his body would hold up.

His loneliness touched me, and I began to drop in as often as I could. We had little in common, but it didn't seem to matter. I sat with him as he talked about his past and his hopes, and listening to him, I slowly opened my heart to what was occurring in his life as he summoned the courage to get through the next hour and the next.

The paralysis spread relentlessly, and finally Jim could no longer speak. But, he remained fully aware, and I promised him that we'd face whatever was ahead together. Sometimes I'd ask myself, "Who is the Jim I'm visiting here? His personality is on hold, his body is nearly dead, our normal channels of communication are shut down, yet I'm connecting with him more powerfully than I do with almost anyone else in my life." Even though he was almost completely immobile, there were moments when he seemed inexplicably happy. And looking into the eyes of this man who had every reason to despair, I'd be filled with a profound sense of peace. He lived to tell me that he felt it, too.

Ancient Greeks believed that a soul's presence could be sensed in a special place, a sacred sanctuary that they called *temenos*. In such places—a temple to the gods, a sea grotto, a grove of oaks—it was possible to feel soul-deep connections to one another and to the Eternal.

I think we often discover our *temenos* at the side of the dying person we care for, and many people have told me about the Shanti moments they've experienced. Some, such as the ones I shared with Jim, happen in silence. Others follow the sharing of heartfelt memories or "I love yous." They open us, change us. I know the "I love yous" I exchanged with my parents at the end of their lives will live within me, and comfort me, for as long as I'm here.

Healing the Spirit with Love

For the dying person, loving connections and Shanti moments can begin to amplify the voice of the soul and soothe the spiritual crises that arise as death nears.

Depth psychology talks about the way we tend to view ourselves from the perspective of the ego and logical mind for most of our lives. Absorbed in our activities, plans, careers, and accomplishments, we happily believe we are what we do. But occasionally, we realize that we are much larger than our logical minds and our preoccupations. We fall in love, feel the immensity of awe, and are moved by beauty or passion that transports us. And with a kind of wordless wonder, we see ourselves through the lens of the soul.

Remembering our larger selves, as we do in those glimpses, is a pressing task at the end of life. The ego alone has no answers for the question of what happens after our hearts stop, and the terror of that can be overwhelming.

Some people can fall back on a strong faith in a caring divinity to whom they'll return when they die, an afterlife in which they'll be reunited with loved ones and ancestors, or a cycle of rebirth in which their essence will live on and on. There's much comfort in that, and it's important to support your loved one in talking about these beliefs, even if you don't share them. I've often found it inspiring to witness the faith of others and felt strengthened by it.

But the nearness of death can also bring people to a crisis, a realization that their previous beliefs don't adequately help them face what looms ahead. This can be as true for clergy members as for those who have, until now, been intellectually comfortable with the idea of death as a final fade to black.

If your loved one is fearful, you can help by first listening from the heart to those fears and then helping him or her discover what sorts of beliefs make sense now. It can be comforting for both of you to have a heart-to-heart conversation, or two, about what ideas about the afterlife speak most persuasively to you.

You don't have to have answers or pretend to believe what the other person does. It's fine to say, "I don't know, what do you think?" What's most important is your willingness to be present with the questions, the belief, and whatever else comes—without trying to persuade, argue, or convert. Against the infinite unknown, you are two people, together, comforting each other with your presence, your friendship, and your love.

Responding to Nudges from the Soul

Many dying people feel the currents of the soul surfacing in the love and peace that arise during Shanti moments, and the moments of connection that put them in touch with something much larger than their individual pain. They begin to have intuitions about the presence of a self that is greater than the body. Talking about what they're experiencing can help them integrate the insights of the soul with what they think happens after they die. Even as their bodies are failing, they can enlarge their sense of who they are.

That was true for Roger, a thirty-eight-year-old philosophy professor with advanced colon cancer. In the weeks before he died, he asked me to read to him from *Pensées,* a book by the seventeenth-century French philosopher Blaise Pascal. Roger had begun to drift into sleep more readily than before, and as he rested with his eyes closed, I was sure I was reading to myself. Then I reached the following passage:

> When I consider the short duration of my life, swallowed up in the eternity before and after, the little space which I fill and even can see, engulfed in the infinite immensity of spaces of which I am ignorant, and which know me not, I am frightened, and am

astonished at being here rather than there; for there is no reason why here rather than there, why now rather than then. Who has put me here? By whose order and direction have this place and time been allotted to me? . . . The eternal silence of these infinite spaces frightens me.

Roger's eyes shot open, and he asked me to read that final line again, then again. I read it to him three or four more times, and each time, Roger nodded his head. "That's it," he said finally. Tears ran down his cheek. "Please tell my doctors and nurses—that's why I'm so afraid."

I held Roger's hand and let him know I'd felt that fear; "the eternal silence of these infinite spaces" frightened me, too.

I've told this story often and recounted the outlines of it in my book *Sometimes My Heart Goes Numb,* but I haven't talked much about what came next. It was a kind of "soul opening."

As I sat with Roger in the days after that emotional meeting, I asked him if he wanted to talk more about his sense of the "eternal silence" that made him feel so small and scared. He felt confused, he said, and maybe if I told him what

I thought about the nature of those "infinite spaces," we could talk things through.

So I shared the story of why I believe what I do, something you might do with your loved one. Such stories, even when they recount a loss of faith or the emergence of beliefs that are far different from your loved one's, can help the other person by providing something to react to or push against—a starting point for clarifying what he or she believes now.

I told Roger that I hadn't been able to embrace religion or spirituality in my early life. My family had felt the terror of all Jewish families living in the time of the Holocaust, and I concluded that life was basically random and absurd. If there had been a divine plan behind what had happened, I wasn't interested in the kind of god who came up with it. I trained to be a mathematician, and I believed in science, not God. Math, not metaphysics.

But as I worked one of my first jobs, I saw something that changed my mind. I was part of the sprawling organization that sent the Apollo 11 spacecraft into space, putting humans on the moon for the first time, and I vividly remember seeing the astonishing photos of Earth taken from space: our blue planet glowing against a velvet blackness. The astronauts—

a crew of atheist fighter pilots—talked like mystics about the grandeur, beauty, and incomprehensibility of space, and I understood why. I felt in my bones that we were witnessing a kind of magnificence we'd never before been able to see.

The awe I felt was beyond words or reason. It was spiritual. I told Roger how that feeling led me to explore ancient truths about God, the soul, and spirituality and how my work with dying people had opened me up to those beliefs.

I wasn't interested in converting him or persuading him. I only wanted to help him explore what *he* believed and let him know there was room to enlarge those beliefs if he wanted to. I told him about a line a Shanti client had handed me: *Help me, Lord, for I fear the path I am on does not go all the way.*

We talked about philosophers who believed there was a spiritual side to human nature and how their beliefs might have influenced their lives and their deaths. I also asked him questions such as "How would things change for you if you believed in God, or in a soul, or in a spiritual side of your nature?" and "What do you think I was experiencing when I viewed those photos of the Earth from space?" And, I took care to keep returning to questions: "What do you think?" "What would you like to believe?" "What do you understand now that you didn't before?"

In the time we spent together with our questions and wondering and speculation, Roger told me he felt less alone, less apprehensive. The soul began to nudge him with a sense that "there might be more to me than this," more than his books and ideas, more than the ego, more than a brief flicker that would be replaced by infinite silence. The fears that dogged him when he was by himself began to subside, and sometimes, he told me, he felt as if he were in the presence of "something larger than myself."

Like many people, he didn't gravitate toward traditional ideas of God or an afterlife, but he found comfort just the same in the feeling of a protective presence, allowing the possibility that he might be part of something more encompassing than his finite body. In a similar way, my mother loved the idea of being like a drop of water during her lifetime that came from a wave and returned to a wave, but she didn't relate to more traditional ideas of heaven or eternity or God.

What I've seen repeatedly is the way the mind begins to expand at the end of life as it incorporates the insights of the soul. For the soul, which is attuned to a sense of eternity, the idea that we are something larger than the body seems entirely reasonable and doesn't require religious training or belief. It's a sense of knowing.

Whatever insights come, your caring support will help your loved one explore the fears and questions that feel so urgent now.

Bringing Light into the Darkness

For all I've said about the power of loving words to heal, I know that words can fall short when we confront the loss and sadness of the dying time. At such times, there are other vehicles for closeness and renewing your sense of hope. Silent prayer or meditation, music, and touch can be beautiful expressions of love.

As you sit at a bedside beside a person who is asleep, or awake but resting in silence, one way to replenish yourself is by making your own connection with whatever life or love or soul you believe is larger than you are. Any spiritual practice you have can support you now, as can a hospital or hospice chaplain. Whatever your beliefs, the following visualization, adapted loosely from a Tibetan Buddhist practice done at the end of life, is a comforting way to bring a feeling of love and grace into the room when darkness feels too close.

Golden Light Visualization

AN EXERCISE

Sit comfortably in a chair with both feet on the ground. Take several slow, deep breaths, and if you can, close your eyes. Imagine yourself looking into a deep-blue sky. As you gaze into it, imagine that a radiant ball of golden light appears in the sky above your head. Imagine that this light is the embodiment of truth and wisdom and love, however you understand it. It can be God or any religious figure who speaks to your heart. You can also imagine it simply as pure, healing light.

As you slowly breathe in and out, let that light pour through the top of your head and stream into your heart. Let the light fill your whole body, dissolving any pain or darkness you feel. Keep breathing, imagining that through this light, you're making direct contact with the infinite source of love and healing. Feel yourself being healed and restored by this light.

Continue for as long as you'd like.

o o o o

You can also visualize golden, healing light above your loved one. Imagine that light is pouring into his or her body, bringing peace and a connection with pure, loving spiritual energy.

Give Love and Let It Renew You

For all the pain that can flood this narrow space between living and dying, there's also exceptional grace. I think and talk often of a Shanti volunteer named Micaela Corazon, who often described what she did as "heart work" and clearly saw it in spiritual terms. She was a skilled massage therapist and sometimes shared that gift with those she visited, hoping to counter the poking, prodding, and pain that are associated with touch when people are ill.

One of the people she drew close to was a man in his fifties, an accountant named Richard who was dying of AIDS. "Richard spoke openly about his life, his loves, his illness, and also death, dying, and suffering," she said. "Our closeness has somehow stayed with me, nurtured me." Richard loved art and opera, and, Micaela says, "Beauty was his God."

When she learned that Richard would be leaving the hospital ward where she'd been visiting him and spending his remaining days in a hospice, she arranged to give him a last massage; his favorite music filled the room as she soothed him with her healing touch. "Playing Maria Callas for him was like bringing the voice of God into the room," she said. "We shared the gift of time together, time spent in real contact, a healing connection that enriched us both.

"I told him, 'I'll miss you when you go to hospice. I feel like we've really seen each other and known each other despite the fact that we've only had a few visits.' Richard could be whoever he wanted to be with me." He wept, and, finally, he let go.

Micaela saw her caregiving—the words and listening, the music and touch—as a statement of love that communicated, *I choose to be with you in a healing partnership. I will stand with you in the midst of despair.* In that connection, she found what she calls an endless well of love.

They May Not Let You In—Love Anyway

Micaela told me one more story about the way things went when one of her close friends, Larry, was dying of lung cancer at age forty-four. Before he became ill, Larry had spent hours with her, watching movies and laughing. "He was like an uncle to my family," she said. In his dying time, it seemed natural to her that they would talk as openly as she had with Richard, a stranger. But, it never happened. "When Larry got sick, there were times when he hated everything and everybody. All I could do was listen and reflect back to him what I saw and heard. I'm a very spiritual person and I wanted to talk with him about his thoughts—and mine—about God, spirituality, and the cosmos. But, he wouldn't do it.

"He was healed somewhat by being accepted as a member of our family, as one of us. But, we could have been so much more to each other. I went with him to treatment—chemotherapy, radiation—and would bear witness to many of the tough things he went through, but he would never engage in deep conversation. It was a seventeen-month journey from diagnosis to death, and the whole way I would show up, pay attention, and always care deeply about him. I would sit quietly and pray for him. I would ask how I might help to heal his pain, spiritually and emotionally. I would ask: if it were me going through this, how would I handle it?

"I also supported Larry's mom, who also didn't want to talk about illness, death, or dying. Denial was the norm in the family, and I tried to accept their way of doing things, but it was hard. I hated being shut out a lot even though I was a close friend. I could have helped a lot more. I've been doing this end-of-life work for many years. I know it was my ego judging how he should do his journey. I wanted him to be different, but I had to be comfortable with not getting what I wanted. He would get close to expressing emotion but then would stop. He was just too scared."

The truth she points out is one that you should know: your friend or family member may not choose you when he or she needs to talk about difficult emotions, big life questions, or unresolved issues. Understand that this may simply be selective communication, not rejection, and not denial of the end that's so close. People may choose someone they feel closer to, or someone not as close, or someone who was there at the right time. It's not uncommon for a member of the cleaning staff or a casual visitor to hear a person's most closely held thoughts.

"Intimacy can come from the strangest people," Micaela said. "What I mean is that sometimes you can connect deeply with total strangers. You can have tremendous intimacy with people you don't know well and then much less closeness with your intimates. It made me feel bad when I saw the nurses get closer with Larry than he would allow me to get. They didn't know him very well, but he would let them in and wouldn't do the same with me.

"The nurses only saw 'a patient,' but it made it easier for Larry to let them in. He shut me out. He was afraid that I would see more than he was prepared to deal with. Maybe it was a strange part of his healing, an expression of his love for me, that he was protecting me from his pain by not wanting to talk about it. And, maybe, he was also protecting himself from the strong emotions that would have come up if the two of us had jumped into the deep part of the emotional pool. I guess I'll never know."

You can't control how close your loved one will let you come. You may be the one whose overtures prompt deep and needed discussions about soul and spirit. However, it may be someone else. Most important is the fact that the dying person feels comfortable and able to open up to *someone*.

All you can do is express your love as well and as freely as you can. As you do, you can find an inexhaustible source within yourself and use it to keep refilling your heart. Then, you can be all you need to be for the other person, all the way to the end. Do it with words. Or with touch. Or with music, or loving thoughts. Let love heal you both.

Chapter Nine

I Will Accompany You
as Far as We Can Go Together

THE 9TH COMMITMENT

In the final days and hours of your life,
I will stay with you at the threshold, knowing you can
feel my presence and hear my loving words.
When you are gone, I will keep our relationship and the
love I feel for you in my heart. You will live on in me.

There's no single path through the dying time. A person with a terminal illness might move toward death for months, even years. Just as easily, a recently diagnosed condition could overtake the body with breathtaking speed. But for everyone, the final stage will come, and for most it will be marked by a point at which the systems of the body systematically begin to shut down, while the mind disengages from this world, seeming to sense something beyond.

The very end is a threshold time, when we can feel the other person's hold on life loosening, as old ways of being and communicating slip away. Please remember that your presence now means everything to your friend or family member. Remember too that your loved one's body knows how to die—it's a natural process. The struggle and suffering that have come before generally subside, and with proper pain medication, most people die peacefully. Your nurturing and support can further ease the way to the end, emotionally and spiritually, for both of you.

Signs That the Body Is Letting Go

A distinct set of changes often signals that someone has reached the final phase of the dying process. You can find a full list in the resources section, and I'll describe the key changes in the following paragraphs, but be aware that what happens for each individual depends in part on the illness involved and the medications being given.

People with cancer and AIDS, for example, tend to waste away and decline in a fairly steady and predictable way. Those with conditions such as heart disease, stroke, or dementia may seem to falter but then come back—and that may happen repeatedly. By contrast, people whose conditions have compromised their lung capacity may die suddenly in this phase. Your hospice and care team will point out the signs they see, but right up to the end it can be difficult to say precisely when death will come. This final period can last weeks—or just a few days or hours.

At the very end, the dying seem to have a foot in two worlds, with gradual, mostly gentle, movement toward the unseen. They appear less attached to who is visiting or might soon come, and they're less interested in the events around them. They often look as though they're asleep, sometimes mumbling a few clues about what they're experiencing, what's coming to them in dreams or insights. If they're being heavily medicated for pain, they may be awake for only short periods.

During this time, they are letting go of input from the outer world, a process that involves losing desires and senses, which happens in the same sequence for most people. James L. Hallenbeck, a hospice physician and author, has detailed that sequence and wisely points out something that's easy to overlook: each of their losses creates a loss for loved ones, as well.

The dying lose their desire first for food, then for water. Seeing someone turn away sustenance can feel distressing, but it's happening not because the person is trying to hasten death, but because he or she no longer feels hunger or thirst. It's part of the natural process of dying, perhaps the body's way of reducing the burden that comes with digestion and eliminating wastes.

This loss of hunger and thirst can create a disorienting void for you if you've been working hard to keep the other person's strength up with favorite foods. One man told me how he'd been consumed with finding melon in the middle of winter because it was the only thing his loved one wanted to eat. And when his partner refused that too, it seemed as though there was nothing left to do but wait and grieve.

It's startling when someone no longer wants to eat, but despite this loss, you can continue nurturing the other person by offering ice chips or small sips of water to moisten his or her mouth. Coaxing your loved one to eat or drink now will only be frustrating for both of you.

Your loved one's ability or desire to speak will likely fade next, though he or she may remain alert. When speech recedes, it can feel as though you're on the other side of a barrier you can't cross, walled off from knowing what your loved one is feeling or thinking. However, you can still fall back on listening from the heart—this time "listening" to body language and staying attuned to facial expressions.

The other person can hear and understand you, so continue to speak from the heart and talk *to* your loved one, not *about* him or her, when you're at the bedside. Your loved one can reply if you take care to ask questions that can be answered with a yes or no—a nod or shake of the head. Keep communicating when speech wanes. I've noticed the way words such as "You're all right. I'm here" can calm a dying person's breathing, and I've felt my loved ones softly squeeze my hand in response to an "I love you."

The senses of touch and hearing are the first to develop in the womb, and they stay with us until the end. Keep talking. Keep offering touch.

Altered States: Dreaming into the Next World

The physical sense that diminishes after speech is usually sight, and you may have the disconcerting feeling that the dying person is looking right through you, without fully realizing you're there. It's also common for the dying to misperceive what's happening in the room, for instance, confusing a piece of furniture for a person.

At the same time vision fades, your loved one may report seeing things you don't. Deathbed visions, which often take the form of seeing dead relatives and preparing to join them, are common. So are "visits" from children and from angels, even among those who are not religious. At another time, these visions might be labeled hallucinations and be taken as signs of mental distress, but at the end of life, something different is going on. My understanding of it, informed by Dr. Hallenbeck's work and my own years of experience, is that the dying are spending increased amounts of time in an altered state that's much like dreaming, outside ordinary reality.

I encountered deathbed visions early in my work on the cancer ward. One day, I sat quietly at the bedside of an eighty-four-year-old man named Jack, who would die of lymphoma less than a month later. He casually turned away from me and began to talk to someone on the other side of the bed. Startled, I sat mutely for a couple of minutes before asking, "Who are you talking to, Jack?"

"It's my older brother Ted," Jack said. "He's come to visit. He wants to let me know that everything's okay with our mother and father, and that they'll be ready to greet me soon."

Not knowing what to say, I blurted out, "But Jack, there's no one there."

He turned back toward me with an exasperated look on his face. "Obviously there is. It's Ted, my brother, clear as day. I ought to recognize my own brother. Don't you see him?"

"Actually, I don't see anyone." That was all I could say.

"Then you should get your eyes checked," Jack responded. "You're lucky. You're in a hospital."

Many others I met on the ward had such experiences, and the vast majority of the time they seemed comforted by them. I learned not to worry in these instances. I visited Jack daily over the last week of his life and watched as his appetite nearly disappeared except for occasional small bites of food and sips of water.

Soon came the other physical symptoms that mark the very end. Jack spent more and more of his time sleeping, or in an eyes-closed "twilight" state. Then, his breathing slowed and became more irregular, which I learned is because as the body shuts down, the normal brain responses that regulate breathing become disturbed. Jack would take a few rapid, shallow breaths, then go for a time without breathing, and then take a few more quick breaths. While this kind of breathing can seem frightening, it's not upsetting to the dying person.

Fluid began to build up in his lungs, making his breathing noisy, a sound often described as the "death rattle." His skin turned blotchy and his hands were cool to the touch. His blood pressure dropped, and his circulation slowed.

Taking in all these classic signs of impending death on one of my visits, I had the distinct impression that Jack was in his final hours. I sat with him, holding his hand and telling him that he was safe, and that we'd be able to keep him comfortable. I said goodbye and let him know I'd valued our time together.

But a short while later, his nurse surprised me by saying, "Jack wants to see you." I dropped by his room only to find him sitting up in bed, eating from his tray and watching the evening news. I couldn't believe it. He wanted to talk.

After chatting a while, I said, "You've made quite a comeback from when I saw you at lunchtime. What do you think is going on?"

"I'm not entirely sure," Jack replied, "but I do know that I've got a lot to look forward to." He smiled and looked straight at me.

The comment struck me as strange, but I managed to ask, "What are you looking forward to, Jack?"

He looked away from me toward the far corner of the room, silent for a long while. Finally, he met my eyes again and said, "Mostly tomorrow. That's what I'm looking forward to. Tomorrow."

I asked what he expected tomorrow. A visit from his sons? Continued improvement in his condition? A new treatment that might help him live longer? He just smiled and stayed silent. Finally, I got up to leave and promised to visit the next day.

I arrived earlier than usual at the hospital in the morning and went directly to Jack's room. It was empty. Jack had died during the night.

"How can he be dead?" I asked his nurse when I found her. "I saw him last evening, and he looked fine."

What I didn't know then is that it's not uncommon for people to have an end-stage burst of energy, a surge of life force right before death. Jack's seemed to allow him a peaceful end, and talking about "tomorrow" seemed to be part of it. When he slipped into unresponsiveness a short while later, he wasn't in pain; he died quietly with his favorite nurse at his side. The last words he whispered to her were "Tomorrow. It's tomorrow."

Balancing Pain Relief and Clarity

There can be a vast amount going on spiritually and psychologically at the very end. Dying people's access to their unconscious is sometimes enhanced, leading to experiences such as Jack's visitations and his premonition about tomorrow.

My time with Jack made me acutely aware of how important it is to strike a balance when trying to control pain and symptoms. Opiate-like substances powerfully relieve pain, but they can take away lucidity at higher doses. Allowing people to have waking-state clarity may involve lower doses of pain meds and more suffering.

It's vital to monitor the dying person's preferences regarding these alternatives and make adjustments if they change over time. Jack wanted as much clarity as possible and asked for lower-dose opiates only when his pain grew intense. Other people prefer as much medication as is needed to dull or eliminate the pain, "even if it knocks me out." What's right is what your loved one prefers.

Metaphors at the Threshold

Deathbed visions are often filled with allusions to the passage that's nearing, as people talk about packing, getting ready for a trip, returning home, or meeting loved ones on the other side. The metaphors seem to provide a way of speaking gently, but directly, about what's to come.

I sat with my father in his final hours, after a visit from his sister, whom he'd last seen many years before. We were silent for long stretches, as he seemed to sleep, but out of the blue he turned to me, eyes open, and said, "Home. I want to go home."

"You *are* home, Dad," I said. "You're in your bedroom in your house."

"Home," he said again, a bit more insistently than before. "I want to go home."

Not knowing how to respond, I started to repeat myself. But then I realized that I was probably listening to my father's soul talking, rather than his ego, and that the word "home" had a much different meaning.

"You'll be going home soon, Dad. Very soon," I said. "Would you rather be home than be here?" Dad squeezed my hand, smiled faintly, and nodded. He stared into my eyes without quite seeing me. I wiped away tears, but to him it all seemed matter-of-fact, as if he simply wanted a change of venue, a journey of some sort.

A number of times before, I'd heard dying people refer to "home," and I'd always wondered if "going home" was a way of referring to the soul's passage as the ego releases its grip. I can't say for sure, but that's how it appears to me.

The Rev. Jan Thomas, a Berkeley, California–based minister, talks about how metaphor—and music—seem to ease the transition. In a video called "Music, Ministry and

Spirit," available online, she describes her work with an organization called the Threshold Choir, which sends small groups to sing at the bedsides of those who are dying.

"Some of the songs we really find powerful to use have to do with crossing the river, taking flight, coming home," she says. "When you can deliver that kind of metaphor through the music, it floats over the situation like a blanket of love." That kind of communication, she says, seems particularly apt in "that liminal space that occurs when life is on the wane, and the next stage is coming."

The simple harmonies of the Threshold singers, many of them composed by choir members, are beautiful and healing, and their music and metaphors have a way of reaching in to expand feelings of peace and safety in everyone who listens.

Music is deeply personal, and a Beatles tune can be as soothing as a hymn. Hearing the music of our past, the songs we've loved—the soundtrack of our lives—seems especially affirming at the very end. My mother repeatedly turned to the familiarity and inspiration of her Beethoven recordings as her health failed, and sometimes as she listened, her fingers would move as if over an invisible keyboard.

Just as it feels natural to sing a lullaby to a baby, it feels natural to many people to sing to a dying loved one. The most powerful music of all, I've noticed, seems to be a loving voice, whether it's speaking or singing.

Don't Worry About "Right" Words—They'll Come

In *The Tibetan Book of Living and Dying,* Sogyal Rinpoche, the Buddhist teacher, describes "the hidden spiritual being" inside us that people tend to ignore, or drown out, in much of life. That's the soul. I know from my own experience how easy it is to ignore that source of wisdom, being mostly conscious of the promptings of the ego, which helps us solve problems, make decisions, navigate circumstances, and process information. But as the body fades, so do old agendas and priorities. This is the soul's time.

The pull toward the soul, as I've mentioned, is what allows people to look back with kinder, more forgiving eyes as they review their lives, and it's the soul's "still voice of wisdom," as Sogyal Rinpoche describes it, that fills the hours at the very end.

It often happens that in the dying time, friends, family members, and caregivers make the same shift toward the soul. Old patterns and agendas fall away, and the words we most need to say come to us: "I love you"; "Everything's fine"; "You're safe. I'm with you"; "We'll all be okay"; "It's fine for you to let go." Speaking such words may be an emotional challenge for some earlier in the process. But at the very end, many of us feel and trust this shift toward the soul, to a kind of deeper, wiser knowing that allows us to find the words that ease the transition for both our loved ones and us.

A friend of mine described traveling to visit a friend who was dying of breast cancer in her final days.

"Ellie and I had been very close before she moved away, but I hadn't been in contact with her recently," my friend said. "I'd heard she was sick, but she was recovering and everything was fine. Then someone called to tell me she'd gotten sicker, and she'd had a stroke. I flew to see her right away.

"Things were pretty bleak when I got there. Her stomach was distended, and she was so still and pale, verging on bluish. She slept, mostly. The nurse said her organs were shutting down. I could sometimes see her grimace with pain as she slept and would call to tell the nurses so they'd increase her meds.

"Ellie was a writer, but because of the stroke she had lost most of her vocabulary. The only words she seemed to be able to say were 'wow' and 'okay.' But she was still in there—her face said everything. A chirpy woman who'd been her visiting nurse came in and told her, 'You're doing fine! You'll be home before you know it!' And as soon as she left, Ellie looked at me and rolled her eyes. She knew. I hadn't known what to say, so I hadn't been talking about death with her. But now I could say, 'Yeah, that was weird. We both know you're not going home.' She squeezed my hand and gave me a little smile. I think it was a relief to have someone around who wasn't pretending. Her husband, Al, was distraught, and he was still talking about 'when you come home,' too.

"I could only stay a couple of days, and she was asleep for most of the time, but I'd brought photo books of English gardens, and when she was awake we'd flip through them. Gardens were her idea of heaven. It was so hard to say goodbye. She looked so small and so ill in that bed.

"The amazing thing is that I had one more chance to talk to her. A day after I got home, I called her room to talk to her husband, and she picked up the phone and said hello. I was stunned. 'Ellie, how are you doing?' I asked her. There was a long pause, and then she said, 'I want to die, but I don't know how.' I have no idea how she was able to speak those words.

"I was so startled I hardly knew what to say. I wished I could say something about heaven, but neither of us believed in that. I just started talking, and the words seemed to be there. 'Remember the gardens we looked at?' I said. 'The ones that looked like the garden you had at home? You can just close your eyes and go there, just let go. Al will be okay. He'll be sad, but he'll be okay. And the rest of us will be too. Just close your eyes and go to the garden.'

"I thought I heard her say, 'Okay.' She hung up before I could say goodbye, and she died that night. I will always be so grateful for that call."

Trust that you know your loved one, and you will know what to say at the end. Many loving and important last words have been spoken over the phone, so if for some reason you can't be with your friend or family member, call and have someone hold the phone to your loved one's ear. The other person will hear you.

If you're secular and don't want to talk about heaven or joining loved ones who've died, trust yourself and your own sense of poetry. I've heard people use words about "stepping into the garden," "being like a raindrop that falls back into the ocean," or "imagining yourself in the place where you were the happiest you've ever been." The right words will come. Our wisdom finds us, and as we speak from the heart, simply and clearly, it infuses what we say with the love and gentleness and grace we want to give.

Trust, Safety, and Peace

Recently, as I was reflecting on the stories of the many people whose dying time I have witnessed, I remembered the scene at the outset of *The Divine Comedy* in which Dante, who will soon tour the underworld, is led through a gate inscribed with the words, "Abandon every hope, you who enter here." I'd always thought those words were extremely dark. Abandoning hope sounds like giving up and sinking into despair; however, I realized that the words "abandon hope" at the very end aren't about despair at all. They're an invitation to clear the way for trust. I've seen again and again that when we let go of the hope that our loved one's dying is a mistake and that it isn't really happening, we free ourselves to be more fully present for the process that *is* unfolding in front of us. We can let our hearts guide us, trusting that doing so will allow us to create a sense of safety and peace in the final hours.

There's a beautiful depiction of that in Laura Huxley's book *This Timeless Moment*. Huxley, the second wife of the noted twentieth-century author Aldous Huxley, shares a moving account of how her husband guided his first wife, Maria, through the final stages of dying and how Laura did the same for Aldous years later.

The Huxleys were interested in hypnosis and hypnotic suggestion, and as Maria neared her end, Aldous sat with her, speaking into her ear, "addressing the deep mind which never sleeps." Maria had loved the Mojave Desert, where they lived, and Aldous asked her to remember the changing light of the desert sky and the surrounding mountains and see that light as an "expression of the divine nature; an expression of Pure Being, an expression of the peace that passeth all understanding." Then he encouraged her to move toward the light and open herself to love and joy and peace, to become one with them.

"I kept on repeating this," he said, "urging her to go deeper and deeper into the light," and telling her that he would always be with her. Her regrets and fears were barriers to entering that light, he said, so he urged her to forget them.

"I went on with my suggestions and reminders, reducing them to their simplest form and repeating them close to the ear. 'Let go, let go . . . Go forward into the light. . . . No memories, no regrets, no apprehensive thoughts about your own or anyone else's future. Only light. Only pure being, this love, this joy. Above all this peace."

Maria died without struggle, enveloped in love and peace.

Years later, when Aldous was in the last hours of his dying time, Laura used similar words to ease his passage, urging him toward the light and repeating the words "light and free." That was the feeling she wanted him to take with him.

"Light and free you let go darling," she told him, "forward and up. You are going forward and up; you are going toward the light. . . . You are going toward a greater love than you have ever known. You are going toward the best, the greatest love, and it is easy, it is so easy, and you are doing it so beautifully."

She repeated such words for hours, until at last he stopped breathing. "The ceasing of life was not a drama at all," she writes, "but like a piece of music just finishing so gently."

I share these accounts not to suggest that you use the Huxleys' words, but because the way they talk about "moving toward the light" echoes the language used by so many people who have had near-death experiences and come back describing their experience of light and feeling at one with something beyond themselves and this world. It's possible that Aldous and Laura were guiding their loved ones toward just such a transformative experience, a connection with the Eternal.

It's certain that they were supportive, loving presences in the sacred space, the *temenos,* of the very end. You can be that for your dying friend or family member. Your words, your prayers, your presence, the touch or music you share—all of these can bring peace to you and your loved one in those important final hours.

Trust that. Trust yourself.

Be Sure to Say Goodbye

Whatever you're moved to say, there's one thing I hope you'll be sure to do: explicitly say goodbye. You don't have to wait for the very end when the person's eyes are shut and you're holding his or her hand—although there's nothing wrong with that. As my father's time grew short, I said, "Goodbye, Dad. I love you and I wish you a peaceful journey." Each of the last three times I saw him, I repeated those words, and each time he squeezed my hand.

Have the courage to say goodbye, even if the tears come. If the dying person sees you crying, you can always say, "I'm crying because I love you." Saying goodbye is a way to normalize and acknowledge the dying person's departure, seeing it not as tragedy but as a "leaving" that both of you are negotiating.

If the dying one is still conscious at or near the very end, you can also say, "Thank you for all you've done for me and all you've been to me. I'm so grateful for having you in my life."

If you haven't been able to do so earlier, this is also a time to say, "Please know that I forgive you for anything you're holding onto that you feel may have hurt me. I've let go of anything and hope that you do too."

I reassured my father several times, including at the very end, that I'd take care of my mother after he died. "Please don't worry about Mom," I told him. "I promise that I'll take care of her in all the ways you'd want me to." These are the kinds of simple, meaningful things many people have told me they regret not having said. And, it's good to repeat such words at the very end, even if you've done so previously.

I don't believe that there's any automatic resolution to lifelong or current dilemmas that comes just before death; however, many times I've noticed a kind of peace that seems to be part of the dying process that feels different from any struggle that precedes it.

Love, it's clear then, is more important than anything.

Amazing Grace

Years ago, I read a quote that I think captures the most difficult part of going through the dying time with someone we love. In his novel *Island,* Aldous Huxley writes about "the excruciating presence of an absence." Those words pinpointed what lies at the core of the fear we feel when we're about to lose a loved one: the shattering awareness that soon we'll be without them.

A Shanti client named Rodney, who was tending his partner Ralph as he died of AIDS, told me he did most of his caregiving as he battled that fear. One night, he was overtaken by his fear, and, intuitively, he climbed into Ralph's hospital bed. Ralph had been in a coma and nonresponsive for days. Sobbing on his partner's shoulder, Rodney gently hugged him. Through the tears, Rodney suddenly felt Ralph's hand squeezing his, a clear expression of support.

"I laid with him for the longest time," Rodney said, "holding his hand and singing softly in his ear."

The next morning, when Rodney went to check on Ralph, he discovered that his beloved partner had died during the night. On a notepad near the bed, scrawled in Ralph's uneven hand, were the words "I love you."

"That final gift," Rodney told me, "will stay with me for as long as I live."

I've always seen that love—whether we sense it in someone's eyes, feel it in the squeeze of a hand, or experience it in words—is what endures. It's been an ongoing part of the dying time as you've listened and spoken and acted from the heart, and I'd like to reassure you that none of that love will be lost or diminished if you miss your loved one's final breath.

Many friends and family members keep vigils at bedsides. But quite often, people die the moment a friend, spouse, lover, or child has left the room. That's given me the sense that for some people, death is something private, something to be entered alone.

Know that the time after death is a sacred period of transition. Take your time saying goodbye; there's no rush to attend to paperwork or phone calls or anything else. Be with your loved one, physically or in thought, saying whatever you need to say.

Let Love Carry You

Losing a loved one tears us open. But it is through a ripped-open heart that love's light can shine through. Rodney's story showed me clearly that during the dying time we're not divided into the strong who are healers and the weak who are healed. We find naturally that all of us in turn are healers and are healed by the love we give and receive.

The love you share now, and will continue to feel, can sustain you. The connection you carry inside will help soothe the pain of your loss. After all, death ends a life, but it doesn't end the relationship that lives on in your heart and mind.

Trust that. Trust love.

I wish you peace.

WITH GRATITUDE

"Gratitude is heaven itself," said William Blake, a sentiment that captures beautifully my experience creating *Life's Last Gift*.

First, I am indebted to the compassionate men and women who care for us at the end of life. Special thanks to those family members, lovers, friends, health professionals, and volunteers who generously opened their hearts and allowed me to bear witness to their truths. Each of your experiences during the dying time helped create this book.

The most sincere thanks to Donna Frazier Glynn, whose skillful and dedicated work on *Life's Last Gift* was invaluable. Donna understood soul-deep why the book was important and worked with me diligently to bring it to fruition. Deep gratitude to her.

To Jeff Herman, my literary agent, for expertly guiding me to this project and finding it the right home at Central Recovery Press (CRP).

To Janet Ottenweller, my editor at Central Recovery Press,

for offering insightful suggestions along the way. Janet's intelligent advocacy and enthusiasm for the project, along with that of her colleagues Eliza Tutellier in acquisitions; Valerie Killeen, CRP's managing editor; Patrick Hughes and John Davis in sales and marketing; and Marisa Jackson, the book's cover and interior designer, demonstrated clearly that, in a personal way, this was their book, too.

To Cindy Spring for suggesting several poignant stories and, most importantly, for understanding that this book is about love and service, loss and suffering, and care and trust. She heard me say many times that *Life's Last Gift* is a legacy project for me and always supported this intention.

To my parents, Sylvia and Edward Garfield; my in-laws, Rita and Chick Centkowski; and my closest friend, Rico Jones, each of whose deaths plunged me into my soul's dark night and collectively taught me more about the dying time than any other experiences.

To Arthur Pendragon and Snooky Spring, whose deaths showed me that it is not only when we care for humans at the end of life that our hearts open.

The only way I can fully thank those kind souls who offered endorsements for *Life's Last Gift* is to pass on to others the generosity they showed me.

To Deborah Lichtman and Darryl Brock for showing me the rigors and rewards of the writing life.

Special thanks to Kaushik Roy, Shanti Project's current executive director, and the late Bob Rybicki, Shanti's former executive director, for appreciating both a founder's enduring love for and ongoing contribution to our beloved organization. Bless you both for caring so much about Shanti's welfare and the clients we serve.

Deep admiration and respect for the thousands of Shanti Project volunteers, clients, staff, and board members for demonstrating clearly that love heals.

Among those who care for loved ones at the end of life, there is so much of deep importance that people think and feel but have not yet spoken about in our families and friendship networks around the world. This creates a special opportunity for *Life's Last Gift* to be, in some small way, a voice for the dispersed and largely unheard caregiving community. If we listen, we will hear family members, lovers and friends, health professionals, and volunteers say, "Something very important is happening out here, something basic to the way people relate best to one another, something that makes it imperative that we give and receive peace when a loved one is dying."

RESOURCES

You can find a useful, up-to-date collection of practical resources on end-of-life issues at the National Hospice and Palliative Care Organization's site, www.caringinfo.org. I highly recommend that as a first stop. In addition, I recommend the following resources.

○ ○ ○ ○

Advance Directives

AARP End-of-Life Resources

www.aarp.org/relationships/caregiving-resource-center/info-11-2010/lfm_living_will_and_health_care_power_of_attorney.html

American Bar Association Resources

www.americanbar.org/groups/law_aging/resources/health_care_decision_making/consumer_s_toolkit_for_health_care_advance_planning.html

Medicare Resources

www.medicare.gov/manage-your-health/advance-directives/
advance-directives-and-long-term-care.html

End-of-Life Planning & Care

Growth House

www.growthhouse.org

Forgiveness

I highly recommend this forgiveness exercise from the Greater Good
Science Center at the University of California at Berkeley:
http://ggia.berkeley.edu/practice/eight_essentials_when_forgiving#

Funeral Planning

AARP Grief Resources

www.aarp.org/home-family/caregiving/grief-and-loss

National Funeral Directors Association

www.nfda.org/consumerresources

Recognizing the End Stages of Life

Hospice Patients Alliance

www.hospicepatients.org/hospic60.html

Support Groups & Resources for Caregivers

AARP Caregiving Resources

www.aarp.org/home-family/caregiving/qa-tool/info-2016/
caregiver-resources-support.html

AARP Grief Resources

www.aarp.org/home-family/caregiving/grief-and-loss

National Hospice and Palliative Care Organization

www.nhpco.org

Shanti Project

www.shanti.org

Threshold Choir

At this writing, there are Threshold Choirs in 119 communities across America, with additional chapters in the UK, Canada, Australia, New Zealand, and Cambodia. Go to their website to find out how to arrange a visit.

http://thresholdchoir.org

Talking About End-of-Life Issues with Doctors & the Dying

Advance Care Planning Decisions

This website, which is based on the work of Dr. Angelo E. Volandes, is filled with videos and tools that will make these conversations easier and more productive.

www.acpdecisions.org

The Conversation Project

http://theconversationproject.org

Updating the Dying Person's Circle & Soliciting Help

Caring Bridge

Caring Bridge provides simple tools for creating a private website where health updates can be posted, creating a central check-in spot for friends and family. Posts can be shared on social media, and it's easy to let the dying person's community know how best to help or visit.

http://caringbridge.org

Wills

AARP End-of-Life Resources

www.aarp.org/relationships/caregiving-resource-center/info-11-2010/lfm_wills_and_trusts.html

RECOMMENDED READING

Awake at the Bedside: Contemplative Teachings on Palliative and End-of-Life Care
Koshin Paley Ellison and Matt Weingast,
Wisdom Publications, 2016

Being Mortal: Medicine and What Matters in the End
Atul Gawande, Metropolitan Books, 2014

Being with Dying: Cultivating Compassion and Fearlessness in the Presence of Death
Joan Halifax, Shambhala, 2009

Closing the Chart: A Dying Physician Examines Family, Faith, and Medicine
Steven D. His, University of New Mexico Press, 2008

The Conversation: A Revolutionary Plan for End-of-Life Care
Angelo Volandes, Bloomsbury USA, 2016

The Death of Ivan Ilyich
Leo Tolstoy, Vintage Classics, 2012

Dying Well: Peace and Possibilities at the End of Life
Ira Byock, Riverhead Books, 1998

*The End-of-Life Handbook: A Compassionate Guide to Connecting
with and Caring for a Dying Loved One*
David B. Feldman and S. Andrew Lasher, Jr.,
New Harbinger Publications, 2008

Final Exam: A Surgeon's Reflections on Mortality
Pauline W. Chen, Vintage, 2008

*Final Gifts: Understanding the Special Awareness, Needs, and
Communications of the Dying*
Maggie Callanan and Patricia Kelley, Simon & Schuster, 2012

*Final Journeys: A Practical Guide for Bringing Care and
Comfort at the End of Life*
Maggie Callanan, Bantam, 2009

*The Five Invitations: Discovering What Death Can Teach Us
About Living Fully*
Frank Ostaseski, Flatiron Books, 2017

The Four Things That Matter Most: A Book About Living
Ira Byock, Atria Books, 2014

The Grace in Dying: How We Are Transformed Spiritually as We Die
Kathleen Dowling Singh, HarperOne, 2000

Gratitude
Oliver Sacks, Knopf, 2015

Here and Now: Living in the Spirit
Henri J. M. Nouwen, The Crossroad Publishing Company, 2006

How We Die: Reflections on Life's Final Chapter
Sherwin B. Nuland, Vintage, 1995

Knocking on Heaven's Door: The Path to a Better Way of Death
Katy Butler, Scribner, 2014

The Last Lecture
Randy Pausch, Hyperion, 2008

Living at the End of Life: Hospice Nurse Addresses the Most Common Questions
Karen Whitley Bell, Sterling Ethos, 2011

The Needs of the Dying: A Guide for Bringing Hope, Comfort, and Love to Life's Final Chapter
David Kessler, Harper Perennial, 2007

On Death and Dying: What the Dying Have to Teach Doctors, Nurses, Clergy and Their Own Families
Elisabeth Kübler-Ross, Scribner, 2014

Out of Solitude: Three Meditations on the Christian Life
Henri J. M. Nouwen, Ave Maria Press, 2004

Palliative Care Perspectives
James L. Hallenbeck, Oxford University Press, 2003

Pensées
Blaise Pascal, W. F. Trotter (translator),
Christian Classics Ethereal Library, 1944

Religions, Values, and Peak-Experiences
Abraham H. Maslow, Penguin Books, 1994

Self-Compassion: The Proven Power of Being Kind to Yourself
Kristin Neff, William Morrow, 2015

Sometimes My Heart Goes Numb: Love and Caregiving in a Time of AIDS
Charles Garfield, Jossey-Bass, 1995

This Timeless Moment: A Personal View of Aldous Huxley
Laura Archera Huxley, Celestial Arts, 2000

The Tibetan Book of Living and Dying
Sogyal Rinpoche, HarperOne, 2012

When Breath Becomes Air
Paul Kalanithi, Random House, 2016

Who Dies?: An Investigation of Conscious Living and Conscious Dying
Stephen Levine and Ondrea Levine, Anchor, 1989